Overcoming Sexual Abuse:

From the Inside Out

Theresa Reiff

Cover art: All rights reserved Copyright @ 2019 by Emma Reiff

Editing first version: Joel Reiff

Self-Published through Kindle Direct Publishing, January 31, 2020

Dedication

To my husband Joel

Thank you for standing next to me and truly meaning it when you said, "for better, for worse, for richer, for poorer, in sickness and in health." It has been a roller coaster ride of a life with you (good thing I love roller coasters) and there is no one else I'd rather have in my car. I love you forever, honey.

So here's what I want you to do, God helping you: Take your everyday, ordinary life—your sleeping, eating, going-to-work, and walking-around life—and place it before God as an offering. Embracing what God does for you is the best thing you can do for him. Don't become so well-adjusted to your culture that you fit into it without even thinking. Instead, fix your attention on God. You'll be changed from the inside out. Readily recognize what he wants from you, and quickly respond to it. Unlike the culture around you, always dragging you down to its level of immaturity, God brings the best out of you, develops well-formed maturity in you.

Romans 12:1-2 The Message (MSG)

Introduction

Never in my wildest imagination would I have expected to write this book. I spent most of my adult life avoiding the subject of my childhood. It wasn't all bad. We went to church on Sundays, where, as a young child, I accepted Jesus as my Savior to avoid the lake of fire. This was explained to me in Sunday School. I never went hungry and certainly did not grow up in a third world country. My siblings and I had fun as kids. From the outside, certainly, our family looked like we were doing well. When other parents were getting divorced, ours were still together and leading in areas of our church. Our lives to the outside world looked one way, but at home, things were the opposite – inside our home things were terrible. My father was sexually abusing me. He wasn't the man people saw in the outside world. His nature changed when we were inside the walls of our home. God graciously kept those memories from the forefront of my mind from the age of sixteen (when I had confronted him) to the age of twenty-one. Then they all came flooding back after a significant conversation.

Everything in my life changed that day. The day that I realized that what I thought my life was and what everyone saw on the outside, was not the truth. Those memories were now in the forefront of my mind and began to permeate every area of my life. My life felt as though it was standing still. When I look back at those days, they are gray and without color. I went from my home to my job and back home again. But the time I spent facing my past brought little droplets of color – hope was restored one drop at a time as I allowed God to point me in the right direction.

Now, my life is one big – BUT GOD - He intervened and changed my life for the better in every way! He has brought me to a place that can only be explained by the love and grace (unearned favor) of Jesus on my life, it is miraculous. Without His divine intervention, without the free gift of Jesus himself, and without the people God brought into my life, I would have committed suicide on the day all my memories came flooding back.

The reason I wrote this book is to help you unlock the freedom I have found. My life is nowhere near perfect, but I'm in a great place now and I want to help you. It isn't easy, but life isn't. It isn't fair, whatever you went through, but life isn't. It isn't pretty, but life isn't always either. BUT GOD – He loves you. He has ALL good things for you. He wants to freely give you the keys to living your most amazing life.

We all have places in our hearts that we have kept locked away. There are things people have done and said to us that hurt us to the point that it prevented us from becoming who we were meant to be. Slaves to our past, the only way to overcome is staring it in the face with God's help.

My journey was tough, but worth it because God brought me to a place where I can now share it with you. I want to encourage you to read the whole book. It contains the steps that God took me through, and I do not want you to miss anything that I have gained. Then if there is a topics that you could use extra focus on – read that topic over again.

Throughout this book, you will find the words "Old Locks" and "New Keys," along with other words pointing to the ways that abuse keeps us locked up, slaves and prisoners to the consequences of abuse in our lives. My goal with these words is to show you how Jesus comes and helps us to the degree that we allow. In other words, you have to take the keys from Him and apply them to each place in your life that is locked up. At the end of each chapter, you'll find lists of the top locks I faced in my journey and the keys that helped free me. My hope and prayer are that you will benefit from mine and find your own – we are all created so incredibly uniquely, so I know you will have locks that I did not and vice versa. However, we all need a starting point, and no one likes to be the first in the buffet line; someone always has to lead the way. Please, let me have the honor of starting for you. Use my locks and keys as a springboard to help you overcome.

Don't read this book without a support system. Find a counselor, friends that will pray for you, and a church with people who will pray for you. Find a pastor who can lead and guide you to Jesus. Choose to believe what I am writing in these pages. Maybe you feel you have tried everything. Even so, it can't hurt to try what worked for someone else. Maybe you aren't even sure you believe that God exists – that's okay. He believes in you.

Here are some recommended steps to go along with reading this book:

- Believe that God is good, and He wants to give you all the good that He has.
- Embrace, that you are worth the effort it takes to face your past – even if you don't feel that way, you can choose to tell yourself this (eventually you will believe this if you stick with God and me!)
- Choose not to be led by your feelings. When we are facing hardship, it is not the time to make major decisions and let our emotions guide us. Don't make any large life changes while going through this process.
- Listen to the playlists I've put together on Spotify and Apple Music (search for "From the Inside Out") on your commute, while getting dressed in the morning, and before going to bed at night. Music encourages our souls, brings us peace, and helps us relax.

I used to try to change my appearance. New clothes, new shoes, fresh lipstick, and a new haircut refreshed how I felt about myself. I was like a bright green tree in the middle of fall colors. Never feeling like I fit in, what never occurred to me was that my efforts were futile. I learned over the years that it isn't the outside of us that needs to fit. We need to work first on the inside of ourselves and then let that reflect on the outside. The best of spa days cannot undo our past, the God of our Universe, wants to change our future.

So, here's what I want you to do, God helping you: Take your everyday, ordinary life—your sleeping, eating, going-to-work, and walking-around life—and place it before God as an offering. Embracing what God does for you is the best thing you can do for him. Don't become so well-adjusted to your culture that you fit into it without even thinking. Instead, fix your attention on God. You'll be changed **from the inside out**. Readily recognize what he wants from you, and quickly respond to it. Unlike the culture around you, always dragging you down to its level of immaturity, God brings the best out of you, develops well-formed maturity in you. (**emphasis mine**)

Romans 12:1 (MSG)

I am praying for you. Your journey may be different than mine, BUT GOD – He is the same. He wants to meet your needs just like He met and still meets mine. Remember, we can do things even if we are afraid – that is courage. You are not alone!

Freedom

free·dom /ˈfrēdəm/ noun
the state of being free or at liberty rather than in confinement or under physical restraint: He won his freedom after a retrial. The absence of or release from ties, obligations, etc.

In the United States, we live in a "free country" where our rights include freedom of speech, freedom to bear arms, etc. These freedoms were gained by the blood, sweat, and tears of our ancestors. They sacrificed their lives so that we could live in a place where we get to decide, in many ways, our fate. I love what Franklin D. Roosevelt says about freedom – we must achieve it!

"In the truest sense, freedom cannot be bestowed; it must be achieved." — **Franklin D. Roosevelt**

This first chapter is about both outward freedom and inward freedom. I will share with you how to break free of your past by giving yourself permission to be emotional when needed. You will discover how boundaries are important to every person's freedom to be who they were meant to be. In addition, we look at common coping mechanisms that may have helped us in the past, but that need to be let go now so that we can walk in true freedom.

Freedom is choice to receive the gift God gives us when we allow Him to work in us. There is work to be done. My prayer is that you will embark on this journey toward freedom. I believe **you** can and will find freedom. If people have fought wars for the freedom of their countries, then you can fight for inner freedom, just as I have. You are worth it, and so are the people in your life that need you. There may be days when you feel like giving up. On those days remind yourself, I am praying for you. If you put your faith in God, and what He wants to do – He will do it!

As you read this book, listen to what God is saying to you, and practice what you are learning - give yourself the time and space to be okay with the ups and downs of the journey. Just like we unpack our suitcases after a trip, we are going to unpack some things together. So, breathe, and allow yourself to be emotional if needed. The following sections cover the areas where I needed to give myself some space on my journey to freedom. Yours may be a little different – that's okay. You can start with mine and God will help you discover those that are unique to you.

The most simple and important prayer I have ever prayed is this:

Dear Jesus, I need you. Would you please come into my heart and life? Forgive me for all I have done that goes against who you originally wanted me to be. I need your help to overcome things that have happened to me. In Your Name, Amen.

I Needed to Step Away for A Season

At the age of 21, I was unaware that I was sexually abused as a child. My memories were all locked up, buried in my brain. In a conversation with one of my siblings, I realized what happened, and then began a process of my memories revealing themselves. It was an overwhelming time. There wasn't enough help, any friend, or any resource that could help me escape what I had to face. I had to walk through it, and I had to face it.

With all the expectations I had for myself, this process threatened every area of the life I was building. I could no longer lead the College & Career group at church. I stopped participating in extracurricular activities and volunteer opportunities. My social life was non-existent because my emotions were so unpredictable. I often broke down into "ugly cries" that kept a lot of my friends at bay. I showed up for my first counseling appointment, full of fear. With no idea what to expect, my counselor began asking me a series of standard questions.

After those were complete, she looked me straight in the eye and gently asked, "What commitments in your life are essential right now?". My thoughts were dizzying. What could I give up for this season? What couldn't I give up? I had to work. I knew that much. Other than that, I couldn't even focus on what commitments I had. She made my life very clear-cut for that season. I was freed to spend time facing what had happened to me. This freedom was what I needed. In the week after that conversation, as graciously as possible, I let people know that I would be taking a break from hanging out as much, taking classes, and volunteering.

Because of my willingness to step away from these commitments, I unlocked space and time that I desperately needed. It gave me freedom to see what I needed to focus on go to counseling, so that I could move forward on my journey toward healing.

You May Need to Step Away for A Season

Are you on the PTA? They will survive if they have to find someone else. For a long time, have you always done _____? Unless you are a surgeon, I suspect that no one will die if you hand off the baton for a bit to take care of yourself. None of us are irreplaceable when it comes to the positions we hold. Say an emphatic "no" to a whole lot of good things so that you can focus on one great thing – yourself. Time is something we never get back. Take this time for yourself is crucial to making progress on your journey.

While reading this book, it might be a good time to ask yourself, "What if?" What if you took this opportunity to put effort into yourself? What would life be like if your past no longer affected your present? What if you were able to thrive instead of striving? What if you were able to forgive those who hurt you in the past? What if you were able to experience complete freedom?

Your season of healing won't be like anyone else's. You may have been at this for a long time, or you may have just started. Either way, stepping back and reevaluating your commitments is worth the brain space and time. By reprioritizing your mental health, you can let those bars that keep you caged fall and step into the most fulfilling time of your life. You can expect God to work in you and through you as as you take these steps, and your vision for the future will expand.

I Needed the Freedom to be Emotional

When I started to face what had happened to me, I was like a wounded bird in a cage. I felt alone and stuck. Once I started to face the bars of my cage, I could not stop crying. For weeks on end I went to work in tears and cried throughout the day. At that time, I worked at a Christian radio station in Boston. What a blessing it was because I was able to listen to great people talk about exactly what I needed. I needed to give myself the freedom to cry. Most of us try to "hold it together." We think we have to whether for the sake of our spouse, our kids, to keep our job, etc. We are fooling ourselves to think that we are doing anything more than stuffing our feelings if we have not faced our past and let ourselves get emotional over it. I don't normally cry, so for me it was a great release. God cares about each tear we shed.

I used to think crying displayed weakness. Even though I was a victim at one point, I never wanted anyone to see me as weak. "Never let 'em see you cry" was part of my belief system. Facing my past changed that belief dramatically. Even though I still do not consider myself a crier, I am much more comfortable showing emotion than I was. It takes courage to allow ourselves to feel the pain we have carried and to be vulnerable.

You Need the Freedom to be Emotional

What kinds of emotions have you felt about your abuse? Have you allowed yourself to feel strongly about it and to cry about it? It can help you learn, as I did, that being vulnerable is not a sign of weakness but courage.

You cannot ignore your emotions forever. In teaching my kids to understand apologies and forgiveness, we talked about what happens when we let our emotions fester instead of talking about them. Siblings argue. It's part of learning to get along with people – the training ground for adulthood. So, I would remind them of that rug – you know the one where you like to sweep your feelings? Inevitably someone comes along and steps right where you had that pile hidden! At that moment, things hit the fan and fly out, hitting innocent bystanders. Our emotions will come out eventually. It's better if we face them each time they do. In this journey toward freedom from your past, there may be times where the emotions feel uncontrollable. That's okay, have a plan. For example, you might make this plan: if I get overwhelmed, then I'm going to retreat to the restroom where I will give myself ten minutes to breathe.

Here's what the Bible says about our tears and their importance to God:

You keep track of all my sorrows. You have collected all my tears in your bottle. You have recorded each one in your book.

Psalm 56:8 NLT

The God of our universe cares about every tear you shed so much that he collects them like a child collects seashells at the beach. He sees each of our tears, whether they would fill a small, medium, or large-sized latte cup. Trying to grasp even one person's tears over a lifetime seems tedious. BUT GOD, who created our whole universe, tells us that He collects the tears and records them in His book! Despite how hard that is to grasp, I believe it. I encourage you to decide to believe it, too. It is one of the ways we can begin to comprehend in our finite minds the love our infinite God has for us.

I Needed to Set Boundaries with People

Dr. Henry Cloud and Dr. John Townsend wrote a book called "Boundaries." This book has been an essential tool for me. Why? Why are boundaries in our relationships so vital? Here's how Dr. Cloud and Dr. Townsend define boundaries:

"Boundaries define us. They define what is me and what is not me. A boundary shows me where I end, and someone else begins, leading me to a sense of ownership. Knowing what I am to own and take responsibility for gives me freedom. If I know where my yard begins and ends, I am free to do with it what I like. Taking responsibility for my life opens up many different options. However, if I do not "own" my life, my choices and options become very limited."

You see, boundaries are just like the deadbolts we have on the doors of where we live. They are there to protect us. They keep the bad out and protect the precious things we have inside. The keys belong to us.

There have been friends in my life not necessarily by choice but by circumstance – we just hung out. I knew them, and they knew me. However, not all of them were equipped to handle what I was facing. It was not their fault or responsibility, just a fact. I had to stop spending time with some of them because of what I was going through. My mind was bringing up so many harsh memories and my raw wounds made me feel very vulnerable. I needed to be with people that I could completely trust. So, some of those people made it through the fire with me, and some did not. It was heartbreaking, but I had to continually choose to prioritize facing what I had gone through over some friendships. Thankfully, I had wise people in my life who advised me to accept that choice.

You Need to Set Boundaries with People.

Remember, the definition of a boundary is "what is me and what is not me." At times, these lines get blurred. But the beauty is that the boundaries belong to us. It does not matter whether you've had them in the past or not. You can create them now. Figuring out where these boundary lines begin, and end is a process. I highly recommend reading the book on boundaries I referred to. Often, it's hard to recognize where we need to add boundaries, especially if we have experienced abuse.

At first, it may feel awkward. Practice ahead of time, know what you will say. Tell the truth. Lying to save face or protect someone's feelings, as we have all done, usually comes back to bite us later. You can tell enough truth to communicate your needs without going into the whole story each time. "I'm not feeling up to being out as often right now; I have some things I'm working through." That is enough. Maybe in the past, you have become used to explaining your behavior. Now you will give yourself the freedom to say these things and end the conversation or, at the very least, change the subject. Remember, choosing only a few people to share with is okay and healthy. We can teach people how we want them to treat us. It is appropriate for our friends to learn to respect our responses without the need for explanation. Ask God to help you identify areas in your life that require boundaries.

Here are some questions to ask yourself to see if and where you need to add boundaries:

- Do you let your boss overwork you? Perhaps you need to add a healthy work-life balance boundary.
- Do you allow people to make all the plans when you go out, but you'd rather make those decision sometimes?
- Do you share and hold your opinions with confidence, or do you feel shot down when you have a difference of opinion with a friend or family member?
- Does it feel like everyone else controls how you spend your time, and you are just blown from one activity to another at their whim?

Start with the areas of your life in which you have felt frustrated. Frustration is a normal part of life, but a constant frustration may be a sign that something needs to change.

I Needed to Lower Expectations and to Learn to Ask for Help

I do not usually ask for help until I am drowning. When it came to the issue of dealing with my abuse, I needed to ask for help. As much as I tried to find what I needed, I didn't even know where to start. At the recommendation of a friend, I started with counseling. Then I added a counseling group. I read every self-help book I could get my hands on. Without seeking help, and instead of trying to do it by myself, the abuse would have remained like a heavy, thick lock. Learning to ask for help brought me to realize I was not by myself, there were people that cared about me.

The last thing I wanted to do was tell people what I was facing. It was an intimate detail of my life that made me feel embarrassed and ashamed. However, walking around in tears called for some explanation. I asked God for help to know what to say so that people would realize I needed space and understanding. As I prayed, I felt like God was encouraging me to be honest, but not share details. I would say, "I am going through some very difficult family issues right now." Or, "I'm seeing a counselor, and it's bringing up a lot of hard things that I'm working through." The second one particularly helped people know I wasn't going to stay a basket case forever – especially my co-workers. It's incredible how compassionate people can be when God gives you the right words to say. I shared just enough, but not all. I didn't nail these conversations every time but having a plan for what I would say helped me avoid the stress of not knowing how to face the situation. Setting expectations and asking for help set me up for success. Taking these steps brought me peace and strength.

You Need to Lower Expectations and Ask for Help

Do you expect a lot from yourself? I bet you do. It's good to have high expectations for ourselves – we will only meet as high as we place them. However, you are reading this book to help you get further in your process; this might be a good time to temporarily lower expectations for yourself. For example, if you are the one who says "Yes" every time someone you know needs help, then maybe for a little while, that duty can belong to another friend. Are you spending all your time with people? In this journey, it may be good to cut back on going out with friends as much. Ask your friends to support you in this season by understanding if you aren't available every time they go out. Are you a workout nut? As good as it is for you, balancing time spent on physical exercise with time focused on mental health care will improve your total health. Do you volunteer for a lot? Perhaps it's a season to allow others to step in where you have faithfully served. Sometimes we keep busy so that we can avoid facing past hurts that keep us prisoners. But avoiding them doesn't set us free. Can you lower expectations so that you can spend some extra time for yourself?

It's okay to ask for help and hire help, too. Are you a parent? Maybe your kids can grab a ride home from a friend's parent for a season. Or how about hiring someone to handle daily tasks and free up time for you? Grocery shop online and pick it up or have it delivered, pay a kid in your neighborhood to mow your lawn, or ask for extra help from family members. It is worth whatever you come up with as a plan to give yourself space to find the keys you need to unlock freedom in your life.

I Needed to Talk

Unspeakable things happened to me. Things that I never wanted to say out loud. To this day, there are plenty of moments that I have only shared with God himself. There were things I shared with my counselor as she asked me the extent of the abuse. What I found was that sometimes, it was useful to share some of the physical hurts that had occurred, and sometimes it was not necessary. As memories would surface, the pain I suffered came back. Talking about this, as hard as it was, helped. Being in a counseling group was one of the best places I did this. There was no need to share the details of what had happened. But, hearing other people talk about how it all made them feel, and feeling understood myself was miraculous. Feeling seen, heard, and understood brought freedom.

You Need to Talk

Having a professional counselor to talk to about your abuse is immeasurable in value. When you speak to someone who can give you the tools needed to handle your situation, it puts you in a place where you are more able to receive help from God. You see, we get in our own way. When we live in survival mode, we have unhealthy habits. In survival mode, we can lock away hurts. These coping mechanisms help us at the time, but later, we need to find new keys to help us so that we can let go of the hurt we experienced. Once we learn how to avoid these behaviors or have someone point out a better way to live, it changes how we look at what God says to us.

Speak to God. If you think He will be offended by anything you say, try reading in the Bible about King David, Jonah, etc. The Bible is full of people who've said and done some ugly things, and God still listened to them and forgave them. He went beyond that and turned their lives around. He has seen it all and heard it all. Nothing you can say to Him will surprise Him, make Him love you less, or cause Him to stop listening. Share everything with Him. He has enormous shoulders and is willing to take from us what we do not want to hold on to anymore.

Carefully consider what you share with the people in your life. Your spouse was not meant to carry what happened to you, so you need to give them the freedom to say no, and you have to decide not to be offended. You can ask – do you want to know? Having an open conversation is worth a few moments of being uncomfortable. Even if you are married to a counselor, their first role in your life is as your spouse. If you are having a financial problem, you do not take it to a person working as a chef because that is not their role. Unless you knew your mailman was also a sound engineer, you would not ask him to put together your sound system. We need to talk with people who are objective and qualified as well as people who love us along on this journey.

Fight for Freedom Well-Armed

The Bible says this:

Put on the full armor of God, so that when the day of evil comes, you may be able to stand your ground, and after you have done everything, to stand. [14] Stand firm then, with the belt of truth buckled around your waist, with the breastplate of righteousness in place, [15] and with your feet fitted with the readiness that comes from the gospel of peace. [16] In addition to all this, take up the shield of faith, with which you can extinguish all the flaming arrows of the evil one. [17] Take the helmet of salvation and the sword of the Spirit, which is the word of God.

Ephesians 6:13-17 New International Version (NIV)

So, if we are to fight this battle for our freedom, what do we need? We need the armor that God provides. First, He gives us protection and then He gives us a weapon! In Ephesians the first armor he tells us to put on is the "belt of truth." Starting with the truth is essential. If someone told you that touching your hand to a hot stove would not burn you, you would not believe that lie. You value your hand. We learned long before we could even read that touching a hot stove is not safe. That truth stuck with us. Now, we need to apply truth to our mind, will, and emotions so that we can fight for our freedom. When we are abused, lies get tangled up with truths, and it becomes difficult to discern the difference. Lies that we carry into our belief system can be as simple as, "I'm not good enough" or as complex as not knowing our true identity. By adding God's truths to our lives, we can begin to sort the truth out. We need truth so that we can evaluate our lives and make good choices.

The next armor we need are the "shoes of peace." When we are walking, our feet go before us and take us where we want to go. Think what it would be like if everywhere you went, peace was ahead of you. No matter what you face, peace is in each step. Peace is in every conversation. The Bible reminds us, though, that these are "shoes" – we aren't born with permanent shoes; we have to put them on! We must participate in bringing peace with us. We receive peace from God by asking for and putting on this armor.

We also need protection for our steps. As we go throughout our day, we have moments where we feel under attack. These attacks come from our enemy (the devil), from circumstances, from relationships, etc. Without protection, we are likely to get injured. However, God provides us with the "shield of faith." Faith believes God is there and will help you even though you cannot see Him. By holding up our belief in God, by trusting Him in our day, we can face whatever comes with faith that He will take care of us.

God also gives us a "helmet of salvation." Jesus' life is our helmet because He gave it in sacrifice for us. When we choose to accept him into our hearts – He can become the filter for our thoughts. Putting on the helmet of salvation also protects us from losing our minds when we feel as though we may go crazy (something I have had to face on more than one occasion). He is the protector of our thoughts! You can ask Jesus into your heart with a simple prayer, "Jesus come into my life, forgive me for my past ways and help me to live your way in my future." As we consciously put on this helmet, we are, in a sense asking Jesus to help our minds stay clear from confusion, from believing lies, and from anything that would send us in the wrong direction.

Finally, in Ephesians 6:17, God gives us our weapon that we are to fight with for freedom. It is the Word of God, the Bible. We need His words, "the sword of the Spirit" in our lives with which to fight. When we utilize His words to fight, no one can argue with them. If they want to argue with God, let them. Remember, you are worth this fight for freedom. Also, when we are already wearing; the belt of truth, the shoes of peace, our shield of faith, the helmet of salvation, and now adding God's word (the sword of the Spirit), we are better equipped to face our past!

Jesus as Our Example

A key example to us of how to live our lives is Jesus. "Jesus wept" is the shortest verse in the Bible, but it is also one that tells us so much about the depth of His humanity. Being both man and God, Jesus was saddened to the point of weeping over his friends' death. Throughout His life we also see Him angry, compassionate, affectionate, and loving. He was not afraid of feelings and was comfortable with expressing them.

Jesus also went against social norms and did not conform to the expectations other people tried to put on Him. Even though He was (and is) a spiritual leader, Jesus spent his time here on Earth with fishermen, prostitutes, tax collectors (the Ponzi schemers of those days), etc. His self-worth was not dependent upon performance. Jesus also rested.

Boundaries were not an issue for Jesus. Even though he had twelve disciples, when He went off to pray, he only brought two or three with Him at any given time. At times He also went alone. Taking time alone is hard in this day and age; we have to be intentional with our time. Jesus did not feel obligated to include everyone in His most intimate times with His Father. No apologies were made or needed.

Exchange Old Locks for New Keys

Old Locks	New Keys
Holding yourself together	**Ask for help** - I can allow God to help me, others to help me, and give myself time to be emotional *Galatians 6:2-3 9 The Message (MSG)*
Having no boundaries	**Create boundaries** *1 Corinthians 10:23-24 The Message (MSG)*
Keeping my past and my feelings about it all bottled up	**Talk about it** – talk to God, talk to a counselor, talk in a counseling group *Job 10:1 (NLT)*
Slave mindset	**Choose a freedom mindset** – "I am free", "God sets me free" – Allow yourself to believe than you can and will be completely free From the Inside out Romans 12:1-2 The Message (MSG)

Moment with God

Jesus, help me to be more like you. Help me to lighten my load so that I can focus on finding the keys I need to unlock Your power in my life. I give you all that I do and ask for wisdom to know how to make space for healing. Please come, guide me, and let me find freedom. In your name, Amen.

Mourning

mourn /môrn/ verb
feel regret or sadness about the loss or disappearance of something.

There is a difference between grief and mourning. Here are some definitions from the website of the Tragedy Assistance Program for Survivors (TAPS): "Mourning is when you take the grief you experience on the inside and express it outside yourself. Grief is the internal meaning given to the experience of loss. You will move toward "reconciliation" not just by grieving but through active and intentional mourning." It is worth taking a few moments to let the meanings of these words sink deep into your mind, will, and emotions. When we understand that there is a necessary outward expression required to recover from loss, we can do what is needed and move forward.

I reached a spot where I was depressed, and I couldn't figure out why. I felt empty, frustrated, sad, alone, scared, and anxious. Figuring out what was going on seemed daunting, and I wasn't even sure where to start. A friend who knew what I had been through said, "Have you gone through the mourning process?" My response was, "Why, who died?" She went on to explain that learning to mourn the losses in our life is a healthy way to process. When people use their sinful free will to harm us, it steals from us. It steals our joy. It steals our innocence. It steals our ability to see and experience the world the way we were meant to. Allowing ourselves to mourn those things we've lost become a key to unlocking and helping us work towards forgiveness.

Facing my abuse, I didn't realize just how many things I would need to mourn the loss of, but it quickly became apparent. As I talked through everything I had been through, it left giant holes. It was the emptying of a bottle of water, as if in a desert, without any source for a refill. Over time, I learned how to find keys to unlock what I needed.

In this chapter on mourning, we look at what we've lost in our lives and how to receive from God what we need to fill up those empty spaces. As a consequence of the abuse I suffered as a child, I lost my childhood and my innocence. Because it was my father that was the perpetrator, I had to mourn the loss of having a good father, or any father, for that matter. I lost the security and providence of having a father. In this chapter, we'll also face together the circumstances in our lives where we need to let ourselves mourn and cover how to move forward from there.

Mourning the Loss of My Innocence

Investigating what I had lost made me realize that innocence was one of the parts of life that I had never understood. I cannot remember a time when I was unaware of how cruel people can be. My eyes have always been open to how badly a person can be treated. Understanding these things at such a young age can taint a person's view of life.

My father stole my innocence when I was a child. This abuse changed my view of the world forever, and showed me at a very young age, the ugliness this world can bring at you. Safe places were replaced with a constant waiting for the inevitable abuse to occur. Pain and fear replaced what should have been safety and love.

When I had my first child, Emma, I'll never forget the feeling of being overwhelmed. Even though I spent eight months pregnant, It felt as If all at once, I was a mother. Her tiny pinkness was a wonder to behold. Emma was born four-weeks early by emergency c-section due to Pre-eclampsia (a condition where my body was attacking my pregnancy). She was only 4 lb. 9 oz. when she was born and initially lost weight, down to 4 lb. 6 oz. Her tiny body fit in two handfuls! Our sweet little baby girl was beautiful, fragile, entirely dependent on us, and innocent. She knew nothing of the diverse and dangerous world into which she had been born. As parents, we knew it was on us to make sure that no matter what the cost, we would protect her with all we had from ALL danger or harm. Having my child made me genuinely question what happened in my childhood. How could any parent harm their child? It was unfathomable to me.

As I parented, I realized more and more what I had lost. My intention to parent well revealed the holes. What was supposed to be a joy-filled time of my life was starting to be stolen as well! Warring emotions were attacking me from all sides. I reached out to God and talked to Him about it. It wasn't an easy process. Letting go of what I had lost while seeing all that my daughter needed was a daily pull from one side to the other. I refused to let the past steal my joy over my daughter and her life. The fight for joy was worth it, and my constant prayer became, "Please, Lord, don't let me mess up my little sweetie." As always, God was faithful and helped me separate the two places in my heart. With His help, I was able to discern the difference in how I felt so that I could experience the joy of motherhood. Also, I was able to offer myself grace with the added understanding of my feelings.

What if I had gotten stuck in one of the stages of grief? The proposed stages have changed over the years, but these four I can mark out in my journey: Denial, Anger, Bargaining, Depression and Acceptance. For me and who I know that I am, I would've gotten stuck in anger. In my nature, I have a temper that needs Jesus' help normally. Add to that, had I decided not to move on through the process, that anger would have turned into bitterness. It pains me now to realize how terrible life would have been for the people who are most important in my life. My husband would've been crushed under my negativity and my children's strength and spirits would've been ruined over and over again. I would have become my parents. The church would have been the last place on Earth you would find me because I would be incredibly easy to offend! My love for people would have dissipated over time leaving me lost and alone in a city where we had no immediate family.

Mourning the Loss of Your Innocence

Just living in the world that we do, our innocence is affected. Pornography itself is abusive – that was never the way God intended us to view sexuality. You need God's help to free you from whatever effects were left behind by the abuse you have suffered. Whatever your reason for reading this book, you most likely need to mourn the loss of innocence. Take a few moments now and ask God to help you identify some areas. Then, feel how you need to feel and talk to God about it. You may need to speak to a counselor about this loss of innocence, as well.

As you read the rest of this chapter, give some brain space to the stages of grief. There are a thousand things in our lives that we lose. Loss is real and has the power to affect us daily.

Ask yourself these questions:

- What stages of grief have I experienced?
- Have I ever gotten stuck in any of them?
- What have I done to get out of that place?
- Should I talk to a counselor about it?

Ask God to help you move past anywhere in this process that you are stuck.

There is an essence to innocence that you can almost see. Innocence is in our world everywhere; in the new shoots of a young plant, puppies, the tenderness of a mother caressing her baby, a baby bird in its nest, and even in the sun rising upon a day. We crave innocence even if we are not always able to acknowledge what it is that we are seeking. When we find it, it can bring freedom to enjoy the simple things of this world with awe again.

Mourning the Loss of My Childhood

There have been times I've heard myself say that I was "never a child." Although meaning it as a joke, there was too much truth. Each time I said that out loud, I injured my soul. That statement brought with it lingering pain. As much as I tried to make light of it – there isn't a lot of humor there.

When my first daughter grew and wanted to play, I found more holes. I was terrible at playing pretend. Since then, I've learned that some of these characteristics are part of my personality, but some stem from never having the luxury of dreamily finding myself in a pretend world. I remember feeling odd as a child, trying to play Barbies with my younger sister, and not knowing what to do with them. I would dress them and brush their hair. Again, I found myself dealing with something that I had lost.

When the first Toy Story movie came out, I can remember crying and not knowing why. My feelings were so strong. I wasn't sure I'd ever stop crying. It felt like I was breaking to the point of being unfixable. What in the world was happening to me, and why would I cry at a lighthearted children's movie? Pixar's incredible way of depicting a child's make-believe world made me realize what I had lost.

Again, I cried out to God that all-too-familiar question, why? Why me? Why did I have to lose something that every child deserves? Was I not worthy of a fun childhood? What was wrong with me? Why me? It wasn't necessarily a smooth, easy process when I had these conversations. Many times, I just needed to get my emotions out, give them to God, and then rest a little before I could hear what He was saying to me. Because of abuse and neglect, I did not have the childhood I was meant to have. God, when he formed me in my mother's womb, did not intend for me to be abused and neglected. His preference is the opposite. The Bible says that He gives us all good things. So, to get past the result of the abuse and neglect, I had to face and mourn the loss of my childhood.

Your Loss of Enjoying a Part of Your Life

Do you have an aspect of your life that you lost the ability to enjoy because of abuse? For example, if you were date-raped in college – you would have lost the opportunity to enjoy living away from home for the first time innocently. Can you see how, when we are abused, it steals our innocence in any season and robs us of enjoying many of life's experiences?

Just as children deserve to dream and imagine, even adults, as children of God, are intended to live joyful lives. God created us to dream big. Do you dream about "someday?" Are there things that you think, "I could do that, if only?" Mourn the loss of the past, whatever joy you lost, let it go. From here on out, I dare you to dream and dream big because the God who created us knows how to create well! Ask Him – He will help you! The Bible says this:

Now to Him who is able to do exceedingly abundantly above all that we ask or think, according to the power that works in us.

Ephesians 3:20 New King James Version (NKJV)

Mourning the Loss of Having A Father

I never knew what it was like to have a father that cared for me in a paternal way. The lack of having that peace, that comfort, that feeling of protection brought emptiness. When I faced the disappointment that was there in my life because of this loss, it was monumental.

There comes a time for all of us that we realize our parents are human. All three of our daughters have seen my limited humanity. They have experienced first-hand my ability to fail over and over again. I have let them down and hurt their feelings. It is a part of parenting – not my favorite, but a part, nonetheless. However, my children know that I love them and that at any moment, if they need my arms of protection, I am there.

In my early thirties, our pastor read Romans 8:37-39 dramatically, and it forever changed the way I view who my Heavenly Father is. I chose that day to replace who I thought of as my father with my Heavenly Father. It was a life-altering decision. From that day, I was able to connect on a much deeper level with God. I knew that He would take care of me and that He always had.

No, despite all these things, overwhelming victory is ours through Christ, who loved us. And I am convinced that nothing can ever separate us from God's love. Neither death nor life, neither angels nor demons, neither our fears for today nor our worries about tomorrow—not even the powers of hell can separate us from God's love. No power in the sky above or in the earth below—indeed, nothing in all creation will ever be able to separate us from the love of God that is revealed in Christ Jesus our Lord.

Romans 8:31-39 New Living Translation (NLT)

You Can Choose God as Your Father

Humans do amazing things. However, we are flawed. We are all flawed. Not one of us except Jesus is perfect. As children, we look to our parents for what that we need. The truth is that parents can't meet ALL of our needs. Sometimes we get confused as children when our parents fail and we may ask, was it us? Did we do something to deserve being treated this way? Of course not. As adults, we need to mature to the point where we are relied upon, no longer relying on our human parents. Life is hard, though. God tells us He is our Heavenly Father and that we can ask Him for anything and that He will give it to us. When we choose to listen to our Heavenly Father for guidance, because He is not flawed, we can live our lives with great wisdom and joy! I encourage you to pray the same prayer I did, ask God to become your Father both in Heaven and here on Earth.

Mourning the Loss of Boundaries

In my journey, I reached a place where I had to mourn the loss of the lines that defined who I was. Remember, in the first chapter, Freedom, we learned what boundaries are, and how they affect our lives when they are crossed, especially when abuse takes place. Mourning the loss of those boundaries helped me to see where in my present life, I needed to add some boundaries (to define what is and what is not me). I gained the understanding that when I have boundaries set, it gives me the freedom to do with my life what I want. Having this freedom, of course, does not give us the excuse to behave badly, but empowers us to make choices with only God's influence.

I had a conversation with a friend that changed my perspective. We were both realizing that not saying no to people was making us miserable. We decided to read the book I mentioned earlier named "Boundaries" at the same time.

As an abused child, I did not organically learn healthy boundaries. As an adult, when I would behave a certain way, negative reactions toward me made me think I needed to change the way I was behaving. The person I became, was a direct response to how I thought other people saw me. The lines that separated me from others were blurred.

I learned so much about what I was missing in my life! Once I decided to start placing some boundary lines in my life, especially in the area of being overcommitted, it brought such freedom. I became free to say no to whatever other people wanted me to do. I had to mourn the loss of understanding boundaries and setting them for myself. Setting boundaries was a key to unlock myself from old patterns of behavior and move forward.

Your Boundaries

Now that we've gone over a couple of times the concept of boundaries in our lives, take a few moments and evaluate the lines you've set in your life. These protective lines need our attention. If you were violated at all in your life, you understand what it feels like when someone disregards your sense of self. Those lines that were violated can turn into ties that bind and imprison us. It is difficult to break free and realign those boundaries. Even if we have loosed them and straightened them, they may still lie askew in some areas. By looking at and beginning to understand where our boundaries are broken, we can see where we need to add healthy boundaries.

Spend some time answering these questions and write out the areas where you need to place boundary lines.

- Can you see how the abuse in your life eradicated your personal boundaries?
- Do you worry about hurting people's feelings?
- Do you have clear lines that define where you begin and end in your relationships?
- Are you familiar with where your boundaries lie?
- Do you regularly re-evaluate your boundaries?
- Do you still have areas where you feel like the lines are more like ties around your wrists?

Setting up boundaries takes time and patience with yourself. Make sure to give yourself the freedom to evaluate one boundary at a time. Applying change to even one boundary will help you realize it is not that difficult. Be brave, speak up for yourself. Each time you do this, be proud of yourself! After you are finished reading this book, I highly recommend reading (or even re-reading) the book "Boundaries" by Dr. Henry Cloud and Dr. John Townsend.

What Losses Do You Need to Mourn?

Stop here for a moment, take a deep breath, and ask God to point out some things you have lost. Trust Him. He wants to fill your empty spaces with His lasting, trustworthy, and loving presence. When we ask, He shows up – every time.

God wants to come and free you from the ties that bind you to your past. When we let him have those ties that keep us bound, we can live more freely. We can take a moment to glance at what we faced in the past so we can go into our future with the keys to a new life.

Don't bargain with God. Be direct. Ask for what you need. This isn't a cat-and-mouse, hide-and-seek game we're in. If your child asks for bread, do you trick him with sawdust? If he asks for fish, do you scare him with a live snake on his plate? As bad as you are, you wouldn't think of such a thing. You're at least decent to your own children. So don't you think the God who conceived you in love will be even better?

Matthew 7:7-11 The Message (MSG)

He wants you to give him all the things that you have lost. Face the pain of the loss and then give that pain to Him. He will replace it with a full heart. The things He fills you up with will fill the holes left from loss. Let Him bring to life all the good He has for you.

Ending Your Mourning

How do you keep from getting stuck in one of the stages of grief? Earlier I explained that mourning is the outward expression of grief. By sharing our grief with others, it creates a place for our hearts to heal.

For me, the process first started to gain forward motion in counseling groups. By hearing other people's stories about what they were going through, I realized I wasn't alone. Finding other people that identified with what I faced helped me to see that I could make it through. Spending time in a place where others understand our pain is a key to unlock comfort.

Another way that I found healing was in helping people. Getting involved by teaching classes at church required me to study, which in turn helped me learn. I made friends with the other people who were there as well. That gave us something we had in common. Along with that, being in those classes created a place where I felt I belonged. My willingness to help other people took the focus off of myself, which helped me see that my current life wasn't as bad as it often seemed.

By spending time serving others, I saw their struggles. This brought gratefulness for my own life and became one of the keys that unlocked my grief. Instead of complaining to God about what I had been through, I began to thank Him for everything I had! I thanked Him for my health and ability to work at my job, which provided pay for shelter, running water, food, clothes and transportation. When something or someone dies in our lives, it leaves holes. If we fix our attention on the holes, we'll have a mentality of lacking. But, when we remind ourselves of all that there is to be grateful for, it changes our focus. When I adopted and attitude of gratefulness, my mourning turned to dancing!

Life from Death

It's tragic when year after year we see forest fires burn. Firefighters get injured and some lose their lives. The fight for survival is exhausting on all accounts. Witnessing the devastation captures our attention, whether we want to look or not. A sad phenomenon. After the fires have been put out, and the firefighters have gone home, a charred landscape is left behind, and something miraculous happens, a phenomenon called "superbloom." Once it starts to rain, the ground produces an abundance of beautiful flowers and vegetation in the exact spot where the fire had been. My prayer for you is that you would experience a figurative "superbloom." That you would walk away from your charred past, let go of things that have died in your life, and let Jesus come to plant seeds in you that grow into beauty.

Here's what He wants to do for you:

Exchange Old Locks for New Keys

Old Locks	New Keys
Loss of innocence	He will heal my broken heart *Isaiah 61:1-7 The Message (MSG)*
Loss of childhood	I choose God as my father *Ephesians 5:1-2 The Message (MSG)*
Lack of care	I will ask God and He will provide *Matthew 7:7-11 The Message (MSG)*
Loss of security	God will make all things new for me *Jeremiah 33:6-7 The Message (MSG)*

Moments with God

God, thank you for always being there. Thank you for all you have done for me. Thank you for never leaving me. I give you all that I have lost. Please take the pain, the hurt, the disappointment, and the lack that is the residue of all that has died in my life. I ask that you heal my broken heart, become my true Father, provide all that I need, and make me full of life and new. In Jesus Name, Amen.

Anger

an·ger /ˈaNGgər/ noun
a strong feeling of annoyance, displeasure, or hostility. An emotion resulting from perceived loss attributed to a willful agent and judged as unfair.

Anger is real. It affects all of us differently, and we express it differently. Anger isn't a sin. Jesus, who never sinned, got righteously angry when he found a group of people making money by robbing people at church. He even acted on His anger. It was righteous anger, not just because He was Jesus, but because He stopped behavior that dishonored God and hurt people. Jesus didn't stay angry. He went back to His regular business of performing miracles, healing the blind, crippled, sick, etc. If you suffered abuse, then that made Jesus angry, too. Anger at sin is right.

In many circles in our society, people think of anger as a sin. Our feelings of anger are real and not sin. However, when we hold on to anger, it turns into bitterness. Often, we forget what we were angry about in the first place. Even if we forget, the bitterness stays. Bitterness can eat away at us, and we need the Bible as our key to remind us to let go of our anger after a time so that we can unlock peace in our hearts.

In this chapter, I'll share how anger affected me. Then I'll show you how I dealt with my anger. I have also included some space for us to look at what makes you angry and how anger can become an incredible motivator when pointed in the right direction.

My Anger at Feeling Helpless

At the age of thirty-one, I found out that my Nana was dying of cancer. She had not been given a good report and spent her last days in a hospital. During her hospital stay, she thought that I would visit. Our family did not live close at that time. I never intended to visit, because if I did, I would have to see my father. But I loved my Nana, so I called her almost every other day to talk. Unfortunately, my father was the person answering her phone, so I had no choice but to speak to him. Because of this, it gave my father the idea that it was okay to call me. At the time, I had no idea how I had let it happen! Speaking to him made me sick to my stomach.

My Nana died about three weeks later. I was sad and happy for her at the same time. She is in heaven with Jesus and fully healed. After that, the phone calls came about once a week from my father and had an ill effect on me. My kids were little, and I was always tired. Dealing with him did not help. I didn't have the energy to set a boundary. There is one conversation I had with my father that I will never forget. He called one day, almost giddy, to share that he had just gotten a new job as the Facilities Manager for a YWCA. At this YWCA, they had a homeless shelter for single moms and their children. Due to his role, he would have keys to every room in that facility. I felt responsible for the safety of those people. My father was never convicted of sexual abuse; he managed to flee the state where it happened, before we could press charges. Therefore, the abuse would never show up on a background check.

My first reaction was anger! How could he take that job? It would be just like an alcoholic working as a bartender! I told him firmly that he should not accept that job and that if he did, I would call the YWCA and let them know what he had done. He refused to listen, and I felt like a helpless victim again. I got off the phone and called my family. We all agreed that we could not let him take that job, and we decided to act. After many conversations and receiving counsel from two different lawyers and our pastors, my husband and I decided that I would make the call. I made it, and we later found out that they released my father from that position.

Even though I felt helpless in this situation, that was not the truth. I found out what was happening, so I was able to do something about the situation. God took care of the rest. I had to use the key of trusting God to make a way for the right people to find out. Then I had to give God my fear so that I would not continue to feel like a victim.

Trust in the Lord completely, and do not rely on your own opinions. With all your heart rely on him to guide you, and

he will lead you in every decision you make. Become
intimate with him in whatever you do, and he will lead you
wherever you go.

Proverbs 3:5-6 The Passion Translation (TPT)

Do You Feel Helpless?

Control is a myth. No matter what has happened to us, we cannot control
our lives. When we suffer abuse, that adds helplessness to our belief system.
However, we can change our perspective, and we can make good choices. Still,
the truth is that we have no idea on any given day what will happen. BUT GOD –
unlike us He does not wake up surprised by anything. He wants all good things
for you and is available faster than the police responding to a 911 call. We may
not be able to control our lives, but we are not helpless. There are some things
you can control; for example, you can control your choices, your beliefs and
your words. By making healthy choices, standing on firm beliefs, and speaking
positive words, you can change the way you respond to the daily challenges of
life. We can choose to ask God to give us the keys of peace and empowerment
and exchange our fear and feeling locked into helplessness.

Anger at My Past Still Affecting My Present

By God's grace, I have three beautiful, amazing daughters! After I had my
third and last baby, the Doctor said I should never have conceived. The parts of
my body that were meant to support a baby, nurture it, and help it to grow, do
not look like they should. Honestly, it was painful to hear even though it
demonstrated how miraculous it was that I already had THREE daughters!! It
made me look again in the face of my abuse, and it made me very angry. Over
and over and over, I have had to envision the whole ordeal. It seemed unfair
and wrong. Sometimes it seemed like I would never escape, when that's all I
wanted to do.

I always thought anger was wrong, meaning I thought it was a sin. Being able
to recall only one instance of Jesus ever getting angry made me think that was
the case. The other people in the Bible that I remembered who got angry – their
results weren't so great. On top of that, most people I encountered did not
handle their anger well, and the results were mostly terrible. But I was wrong –

it is okay to be angry, but it's not okay to take that anger out on someone else! Grab a pillow and scream into it by yourself in your bedroom if you have to – but don't inflict your wrath on another living thing.

When we are hurt, it makes us angry. Abuse of any kind robs us of our fundamental human rights. God created us in his image and intended for us to live a life free from the negative impacts of sin. When we are the victims of someone else's sin, then it is right to be angry! It's what we do with that anger that can make or break us. And here's something to think about – being angry about something won't change the past. But letting ourselves be angry for a time, working through it, and moving on will change our future.

Does it Make You Angry – Your Past Still Affecting Your Present?

There are consequences of the abuse we experienced, and this can leave us angry. Memories of our past can come into our present so easily. Feeling angry about this is justifiable and makes sense! But how can we stop it from ruining our present? We need God's help to get the resources we need. Having a plan for what to do when our past comes back and invades our present is essential. You need tools and resources. If this happens to you, scheduling a time each week to meet with a counselor is essential to give you the opportunity to talk it through. I also highly recommend putting notes to yourself up wherever you spend a few moments every day. For example, above your sink put up a note with the words, "I AM SAFE." When you wash dishes, this will help you remember that you are no longer back in the past. Add some deep breathing exercises to your day – it is an incredible way to focus on the simple goodness of air!

You can find breathing exercises at this link to WebMD:

https://www.webmd.com/balance/stress-management/stress-relief-breathing-techniques#1

Having a plan in place to handle our feelings about our past when they hit us is crucial, and when practiced, will lead us to heal.

I Was Angry About Feeling Isolated

Sixth months after I was married, my new husband and I moved to the Seattle, Washington area. We moved so that my husband could take his dream job at a computer game company. The move was not my favorite. Honestly, it took me five years to change my attitude. God showed me again and again that he brought us to Seattle for a bigger purpose than Joel's career. I admit – I am stubborn! However, that stubbornness over my lifetime has, by God's grace, translated into the tenacity that gave me staying power when times were tough. Thank you, Jesus! In Seattle, I experienced feelings of loneliness I had never dealt with before. I got pregnant with our first daughter, and that only added to my isolation. It drove home for me even more that we were living in a state where we barely knew anyone. We were not part of a community.

BUT GOD - He had not forgotten me and led us to The City Church (now Churchhome) in Kirkland, Washington. This is the place where I found connections with people that truly cared. I made friends. While nursing my baby, I met like-minded women. Signing up to volunteer, I met more friends in the same stage of life as me and some others that had older kids. Having a community, people who understood where I was at and what I was dealing with as a new mom, saved me. It freed me from isolation, but it didn't happen accidentally, I had to want it, and I had to be open to God's leading to find it.

Does Isolation Keep You in Your Head?

Do you think you're better off without others? This belief will lead to isolation. Your enemy (the devil) is always telling you lies - that no one will like you, that you don't belong. Choose not to believe the lies! If we choose isolation over relationship it can result in many types of serious mental health issues. Everyone feels isolated at times. We are all looking for a spot at the proverbial lunch table and need to belong somewhere. Get out, find a group, and if the first one you try doesn't work, try again. Keep trying until you find your place, and you find "your people." Keep an eye out for others that also need to belong and bring them along with you. You don't need people exactly like you – they do not exist. Ask God to lead you to the right people, and He definitely will.

Anger at Feeling Trapped

When I was a young girl, a family member made the statement about me that I'd be "barefoot and pregnant in the kitchen in no time." From then on, that is how I saw myself. The memory of this conversation left me feeling valued only for my ability to produce offspring. Whether or not this was true didn't matter – I chose to believe this was my only value. Then that day came, when I happened to be pregnant, barefoot, and in the kitchen. When that realization hit me – I crumbled. What should be a joyful, wonderful experience (expecting a baby) was turned into anger. I faced a hard couple of weeks of depression at that point. Anger, hurt, resentment; they become my companions.

I have a dear friend in Seattle named Bonnie. She has this sweetness about her, just like Jesus. Talking with my friend changed my perspective. She was like Jesus to me so many times in those days as I saw how much she loved her kids and loved being their mom. Over coffee, we talked about the eternal value of mothering – this was a one hundred and eighty-degree turn from where my feelings had been. These conversations reminded me that my children are a blessing. Honestly, I don't think I even shared with Bonnie exactly what I had been going through, but I let God heal me through our conversation. As we shared month after month about what was going on in our lives, it helped me realize that I was no longer trapped. Our conversations about how God was helping us became a lifeline for me.

Do You Ever Feel Trapped?

Maybe you have been in the same job that you don't like for too many years now. Have you ever considered that you do not have to stay there? Have you always said yes to something because others expect that you'll do it, even though you are no longer passionate about it? Are there things you do because you "always have"? We often let fear keep us trapped.

Or maybe you are like me, and you need a new perspective? Do you have a friend that may have a different perspective than you do? Maybe they have tried to share their opinions, and you have thought they were wrong. Ask God to show you the people in your life from whom you need to accept advice. Look for a mentor-type person that can give you godly advice for life. My mentor has the exact opposite of my personality, but it makes a huge difference when I listen. You could find a mentor or life-coach to help you get a different perspective. God will provide people that He will speak to you through. Fresh perspective – we all need to get it!

Have you ever hiked up a mountain? When standing at the bottom, it seems like a daunting task — with one careful step at a time, you reach the top. As you reach the crest, your hard work pays off and the benefit is an incredible view. When looking at the mountain from the bottom, reaching the top seems too large to accomplish. By putting one foot in front of the other, one step at a time, they all add up to making it to the top, and once you are on top of the mountain, your perspective changes. Sometimes, it just takes putting one foot in front of the other to get a different perspective.

Add this to your "to-do" list: *Change my perspective!* No matter what you feel trapped in, you can step back and review the decisions you've made, the commitments you have, the expectations you've set, or those you have let someone else set for you. Take an inventory – if you feel trapped, give it to Jesus and see what He will do. Surrender any anger you have about it to Him, and He will bring you a fresh new perspective.

Anger Can Be a Tool We Use

Do you struggle with angry outbursts? Is that anger pointed toward anyone present in your life? Have you talked through your feelings with someone when you aren't in the midst of anger? Here is an excerpt from an article from the website **emotionalcompetencies.com**, with a list of the benefits of anger!

Benefits and Dangers of Anger
Here are some of those benefits:
- *Anger tells us that something needs to change.*
- *Anger can provide the motivation to constructively change whatever it was that caused the anger. It can energize the fight for legitimate rights. It contributed to eliminating slavery and apartheid, and lead to women's suffrage and civil rights. Anger can motivate us to overcome oppression and topple a tyrant.*
- *Anger can provide the motivation to constructively correct an injustice. It urges us to act on our sense of justice.*

- *Anger can provide the motivation to constructively teach offenders what they did to make you angry, and to learn to act differently.*
- *Anger can help to reduce or overcome fear and provide the energy needed to mobilize needed change.*
- *Anger sends a powerful signal that informs others of trouble. It notifies the offender that you have perceived an offense.*
- *Anger helps us to preserve our ego and think good of ourselves.*
- *Anger is a normal response to an external stimulus that needs to be addressed.*
- *One of the most dangerous features of anger is that expressing anger increases the anger of others. This can lead to a rapid and dangerous escalation. We may try to harm the target of our anger. We often wish them harm. The impulse to harm is probably a central part of the anger response for most people. While anger can be dangerous and must be constrained, it cannot and should not be eliminated.*

You can find the full article here:

http://www.emotionalcompetency.com/anger.htm

What I find incredible about this list is that I can relate to all those benefits of anger. I realized as I read them that they described exactly how my anger fueled my behavior, in many cases. I utilized my anger to drive me toward solutions. Anger can be an excellent motivator. It motivated me to go to counseling and set goals. It motivated me to read every single book I could find about sexual abuse. My anger became less about *who* I was angry at and more about *what*.

Are there times you have used your anger for motivation, or could you do it more often? Allow the hurt you've experienced, and the anger resulting from it motivate you to find answers and get help. Choose to utilize those feelings to head in the right direction. Here is what the Bible says:

But don't let the passion of your emotions lead you to sin! Don't let anger control you or be fuel for revenge, not for even a day.

Ephesians 4:26 The Passion Translation (TPT)

Moving on From Anger

Moving past anger takes intention. Finding things that you enjoy doing is imperative. Hobbies aren't a waste of time, as I once thought. When you give yourself time to pursue activities that you enjoy, it helps you lighten up. When we suffer under abuse, it is serious, and for a season, our past needs our attention. However, even while we're dealing with it, we need to allow and encourage ourselves to find things we enjoy!

Peter's Anger for Jesus

Human beings have emotions. The men who followed Jesus, His chosen disciples, were human. Jesus was regularly correcting them about their reactions to different circumstances. Toward the end of Jesus' days here on Earth, Peter had an outburst of anger. Note how Jesus handles Peter's outburst.

When those with him saw what was happening, they said, "Master, shall we fight?" One of them took a swing at the Chief Priest's servant and cut off his right ear. Jesus said, "Let them be. Even in this." Then, touching the servant's ear, he healed him.

Luke 22:49-51 The Message (MSG)

Jesus does not get on Peter's case for his anger and doesn't even prevent what happens. Instead, He steps in and heals. Peter loved Jesus, and just as we would stick up for our friends, he was sticking up for his. Jesus understands why we feel the way we do, and He does not condemn us for our reactions, but He comes along and heals what is hurting. There is so much hope for us in this story. I've been in Peter's place. I've lost my temper and hurt someone, though I haven't cut off anyone's ear. If you have anger that has overwhelmed you in any way, you can ask Jesus to come and heal the consequences. He will help you learn how to work through your anger too.

Exchange Old Locks for New Keys

Old Locks	New Keys
Anger at feeling controlled by the past	**I surrender** – my past, present, and future to God and receive peace *Jeremiah 29:11 (NIV)*
Anger at feeling isolated	**I stay connected** – to Jesus and the people He places in my life *Galatians 6:2 (TPT)*
Anger about feeling trapped	**I can enjoy life with God on my side** – I can enjoy wide open spaces, and get a good perspective with His help *Romans 8:31 (TPT)*

Moment with God

Jesus, please help me not to let my anger out in a way that is hurtful to others. Thank you that in those times that I am angry, you will help me to know when and how to let it go and move on. Help me to see what the root cause of my anger is so that I can also give those hurts in my life to you. Please help me to remember that you take care of me. I trust you, God. In Jesus' name, Amen (let it be so).

Know Your Enemy

en·e·my /ˈenəmē/ noun
a person who is actively opposed or hostile to someone or something.
synonyms: foe, adversary, opponent, rival, nemesis, antagonist, combatant, challenger, competitor

We have an enemy. The devil is our enemy. His goal is to steal, kill, and destroy all that God has for us. God's plan is for us to live joy-filled lives. If we deny that we have an enemy, then he can attack us, and we have no defense. If we assign blame to the wrong enemy, we create a new battlefront, also one with no defense, one that is lose-lose for both sides. We need to face our real enemy headfirst and fight using the best weapons. We may still lose a battle along the way, but with God within us, and when we allow Him to fight for us, we will win the WAR. Here is what the Bible says:

> The thief's purpose is to steal and kill and destroy. My purpose is to give them a rich and satisfying life.

John 10:10 New Living Translation (NLT)

The thief is the devil – he will come against us any chance he gets. Again, his goal, his purpose is to steal, kill, and destroy all that God has intended to be good in our lives. BUT GOD - His purpose is to give us a rich and satisfying life. I love that this verse shows that God has the last word! This is the truth, no matter what the devil has done, tries to do or will do in the future, God will always make a way for it to work out for us when we invite Him into our lives!

In this chapter, we will look at the ways our enemy wants to come against us. We will consider what he has stolen and what God will do to help us. Then we will learn about things our enemy has tried to kill in us. Lastly, we will look at what he has tried to destroy that God will restore for us.

The Enemy Tried to Steal My Joy

As a result of the abuse I faced, my counselor diagnosed me as having PTSD (post-traumatic stress disorder). It brings with it a sense of readiness for something bad to happen at any minute. For most of my past, I lived in fear. I was afraid of so many aspects of life that it would be too many to list. However, if you had met me, you would not have known because I was not open about it. I was having a constant conversation with fear, and it won out when it came to choices I needed to make. I was not just a captive; fear was my dearest friend, and I did not know how to survive without it. The abuse that I suffered and the silence about it that was locked deep inside of me kept me handcuffed to fear. Anytime I would try to loosen those chains, fear would remind me of my place.

On any given day at my workplace, I would make mistakes as we all do; small mistakes, such as providing someone incorrect information, or big ones, such as making a decision that cost our non-profit a lot of money. I collected those mistakes in my mind. It was like I had a collection jar that I filled every time I made a mistake no matter the size. At any point in the day, especially if I found myself enjoying what I was doing or someone's company, I would open that jar in my mind. I would remind myself that I should not be allowed to enjoy myself because of my past mistakes. It was a terrible way to live my life. I was miserable on the inside. Continuing in this thought process over many years stole my joy, over and over and over again. I was afraid to enjoy my life because deep down, I was sure that I did not deserve it.

One day while I was sitting in church after worship and during the announcements, I heard God's voice. He asked gently, "Why do you rob yourself of the joy I have for you?" I knew what He was addressing. He continued speaking to me, "Do you think you deserve that? Don't you think that my love for you is bigger than what you are doing to yourself? You are allowing things to be stolen that I have given you because you have not given me your mistakes. You have my permission to let go of your jar of mistakes. Choose to let me fight your battles and stop reminding yourself of your mistakes. What my Son did on the cross for you is enough. I am enough. We can overcome this together." As tears rolled down my face, I nodded my head and accepted what my Heavenly Father was offering. I received freedom from the years of beating myself up. Indeed, it was that simple! I admit there were days where I was tempted to pick that habit of collecting mistakes back up, but I chose to remind myself of that encounter.

What Has the Enemy Stolen or Tried to Steal from You

We feel immediately violated when someone steals from us. Has anyone ever stolen your stuff? When it has happened to me, I felt lost, hurt, and confused. I ask myself, "Why did this happen to me?" Rape, molestation, and abuse in any form steal so much from us. When we are abused, it can steal our ability to trust; it can steal our confidence, it can steal our self-worth, it can steal our ability to love fully, etc.

Take a few minutes, take a deep breath, and let some quiet moments pass. Now, ask God to point out areas where important things have been stolen from you. Allow Him to show you so that you can open up and receive help and healing from Him. If at this time, it is too hard to face, that is okay; this is not a pass/fail test. Talk to God about it – He is ready and willing to help whenever you are ready. If you are afraid even to start this process, that's okay. Share your fear with Him – he is your most patient friend. No one has as much patience as God.

> God is a safe place to hide, ready to help when we need him. We stand fearless at the cliff-edge of doom, courageous in seastorm and earthquake, Before the rush and roar of oceans, the tremors that shift mountains. Jacob-wrestling God fights for us, God-of-Angel-Armies protects us.
>
> *Psalm 46:1-3 The Message (MSG)*

The Enemy Comes to Kill

My oldest daughter Emma is amazing. Since the day she was born, the enemy has tried to kill her. She was delivered by emergency c-section with very little amniotic fluid left for her survival. She was born prematurely. As a small child, she caught every cold, infection, etc. that came along. At one point, she even had a kidney infection to the point that she couldn't walk. As a young adult, things became more difficult and more serious. She began to fall into depression. At first, this was sporadic. Once we moved to Austin, TX, and she started in a new school, her mental health went down hill. Her depression increased to dangerous levels, and she became suicidal. It became a fight for her life. I understood how she was feeling because I remembered feeling that way when I faced my abuse. But, I'm her mother – my first job was, and is, to keep her alive! We made new rules – we hid dangerous items – we put her on medication – she saw a counselor and a psychiatrist. We would do anything needed to save her life. I sat with her for hours, reminding her of who God made her and that she could not let the enemy win. She had to choose her life. I pleaded with her, and I pleaded with God, sometimes all night long. I refused to give up. I am so thankful that I never gave up on Emma and that God did not give up on her either. Recently, she told me that what finally turned her around was that Jesus said to her, "I've done all I can to help you, you have everything you need, you now have to decide to accept my help." Our enemy is real and wants us dead, BUT GOD is a big God who loves us and is ready to help us – all we have to do is accept it!

Your Enemy Comes to Kill

Have you had a season like this in your own life? You have a real enemy who wants to kill you and all the goodness in you. Do you ever feel unimportant? That is the enemy trying to kill God's purpose for you. Do you ever feel like you can't do anything right? If you only look at your mistakes and weaknesses, it keeps you from seeing your strengths. Do you have dreams of using your talents that are unfulfilled? God made you with a purpose and a plan! He wants to fulfill your dreams and give you all that He has planned for you. It is never too late!

God will pursue you relentlessly. He hasn't given up on your dreams, even if you feel they have died. Be courageous enough to ask Him to bring those things back to life that you thought were dead. Just as Jesus raised Lazarus back to life here on Earth, He is praying for you to have a full life again! He is always thinking about you!

For I know the thoughts that I think toward you, says the Lord, thoughts of peace and not of evil, to give you a future and a hope.

Jeremiah 29:11 New King James Version (NKJV)

The Enemy Came to Destroy My Crucial Relationships

At many points in my marriage, the enemy attacked our relationship. The lies I was tempted to believe often outweighed the truth. There were many times when I fell for the enemy's tricks. I saw my spouse as my enemy when the truth was that he is a gift to me in every way. When I met Joel, I felt acceptance and connection to someone like I had never felt. He just got me. We would spend hours talking about anything and everything. He made me laugh. After finding out about what I was facing, he was not intimidated or scared off as I expected him to be. The kindness I saw when he looked at me both frightened me and comforted me all at once. Part of me questioned my worthiness. Thankfully, he did not give up on me! I was not an easy nut to crack! So, how did I forget these feelings at times along the way in marriage? I got distracted. We have to recognize that if our enemy can destroy our crucial relationships, then he can destroy one of the essential parts of our lives. There is strength in numbers.

It's better to have a partner than go it alone. Share the work, share the wealth. And if one falls down, the other helps, But if there's no one to help, tough!"

Ecclesiastes 4:10 The Message (MSG)

Stop the Enemy from Destroying Your Crucial Relationships

What are your crucial relationships? Are they broken? Do you need to remind yourself of why you first began that relationship? We are forgetful creatures. BUT GOD does not forget. Ask God to help you.

Jesus is your most vital relationship. No matter what you have thought or think of Him, He is there waiting for you to share your life with Him – every minute of every day. He will never leave you or change His mind about how much He loves you! Taking a stand for the most crucial relationships in our lives is important. Do you need to rebuild key relationships with parents, stepparents, foster parents, or siblings? Our enemy is always trying to convince us this is more difficult than it is. By taking little steps of reaching out, saying we are sorry if needed, giving forgiveness, etc. we can invite God to help us bring healing to our crucial relationships. These are the people God gave us and the relationships that our enemy has tried to destroy. God can bring life back! Remember, Jesus is your most crucial relationship.

The Nature of the Enemy

There is no battle that God won't win. We might lose some battles, but with God, we will win the war! I cannot emphasize enough that the devil does not have the same amount of power as God does. Make no mistake. The devil may get away with distracting you, misinforming you, creating illusions, so you think one way or another, BUT GOD will always win. His power is infinitely more. God is our Creator. He is the Author of your story, so don't let yourself believe that the enemy has any power over you. Can he come against you? Yes. Will he? Yes, you can bet on it. However, with Jesus praying for us and God on our side – we win. Here's what the Bible says:

> What then shall we say to these things? If God is for us, who can be against us?

Romans 8:31 New King James Version (NKJV)

Your enemy tries to keep you a slave to the lies that he tells you. You need to replace those lies with new keys of truth that you decide to believe. If any of these below apply to you, grab hold of them and allow them to change how you think about your past and yourself.

Lies the Enemy Convinces Us Of	The Truth
It was my fault and I deserved it	Abuse is never your fault!
I don't deserve a good life	God has come to give you a life full of abundance!
I'm not worthy	You are God's absolute treasure!
I'm not enough	God is always enough and with Him you are enough!

I am not qualified	God has chosen you and qualified you!
I am a nobody from nowhere	You are God's cherished child!
No one can help me	God is present and ready to help whenever you ask!
God can't possibly love me	His love for you is wider, deeper, and greater than you could ever imagine or hope for!
God let this happen to me	No – someone took out their sinful nature on you BUT GOD did not want this to happen to you!
I can never recover; I am permanently broken	God will heal you when you surrender your past to Him!
I can no longer be the person I was meant to be	God will restore you and give back what you lost ten-fold!

Make a Plan to Combat Your Enemy

So how do you combat this enemy that we all have? How do we fight this battle when we can't even physically see our enemy? One way I fight is by playing music. All kinds of music. But truly worship music is my favorite. Usually, I get stuck on one favorite for a time that I replay over and over. I love anything I can move to, raise my hands, and get my mind off of things in my day that our bugging me. So, turn up the volume and enjoy whatever music helps you to realize that there is way more to this life than our past and lots of our future left to dance.

The other tool I use to help free me from attacks of the enemy is arming my mind, like arrows in a bow, with scripture. I'm not great at spending hours memorizing, but I do have a ton of scripture verses memorized. My secret? I put scripture up everywhere that I stop. Near my stovetop, on my fridge, and anywhere I can stick a little note from God. Then when the enemy comes and tries to distort whatever good thing has come along, my mind is armed with God's words of life!

Place these words on your hearts. Get them deep inside you. Tie them on your hands and foreheads as a reminder.

45

Teach them to your children. Talk about them wherever you are, sitting at home or walking in the street; talk about them from the time you get up in the morning until you fall into bed at night. Inscribe them on the doorposts and gates of your cities so that you'll live a long time, and your children with you, on the soil that God promised to give your ancestors for as long as there is a sky over the Earth.

Deuteronomy 11:18-21 The Message (MSG)

A Battlefront Example

There are many stories of good vs. evil – enemies fighting for their rights to land, enemies fighting for domination each other – good vs. evil, right vs. wrong. We all choose sides. I love the story of David vs. Goliath. I'm a fan of the underdog and often root for underdog teams. The comeback, the long shot, the unlikely victor always catches my heart, even if my allegiance makes no common sense by the numbers. I'll get on board and stay there until the very last second. My faith is not only durable but committed. So was David's. His faith in God was so strong that, without coverage or protection of any natural kind, he faced a literal giant. David's qualifications did not include battles that he had already won, but he had defeated a lion and a bear. David had no title except brother and shepherd at this point in his life. He was not King at this point and had not yet written the Psalms. He had no claim to fame and was just a kid. You can read the whole story in the Bible in the book of 1 Samuel 17:1-54.

It was an epic battle between the Israelites (the good guys, i.e., God's chosen people) and the Philistines (bad guys). The Philistines came equipped with their "champion," all of almost ten feet of him! The Israelites were the clear underdogs.

Here are the "stats:"

Goliath the Philistine	Versus	David the Israelite
10 feet tall	Vs.	Normal sized boy
126 lb. of armor	Vs.	No armor

15 lb. spear tip	Vs.	Five smooth stones and a slingshot
Kept an entire army at bay twice a day for 40 days with just his words and fierce appearance alone	Vs.	Fought and killed lions and bears with his bare hands to protect his sheep
Cursed David by his false gods	Vs.	God on his side

What caused this battle to end? What enabled the Israelites to overcome this taunting Philistine? Was it David's great skill at choosing the perfect small smooth stone? Had he practiced for hours trying to hit a ten-foot moving target squarely in the forehead? No, not at all. His faith in a God, who shows up when we need Him every time – that is what brought about this unlikely victory. This young boy set aside fear and choose faith in God. It's obvious; He made the right choice. The last we see of Goliath is him being beheaded by David with Goliath's sword!

Put Fear in Its Place

We all face fear. My kids grew up hearing me say over and over again, "You can do things even if you are afraid – that's bravery." Without fear, there is no need for courage. If hearing that we have a real enemy who wants to steal from you, attempt to kill you and is out to destroy you scares you, welcome to the club. Did you know that "fear not" is stated three hundred and sixty-five times in the Bible? Once for each day of a year! That is certainly not by accident. Be encouraged, God is on your side and when you are on His team you ALWAYS win! We can overcome fear with faith. The Bible says this:

> Such love has no fear because perfect love expels all fear. If we are afraid, it is for fear of punishment, and this shows that we have not fully experienced his perfect love.

1 John 4:18 New Living Translation (NLT)

Have you ever noticed how large (or giant!) our problems can seem? When we let fear fester, it turns our trauma, tragedy, and even small issues into much larger beasts. Here is where our enemy does his best work. By holding on to these fears, we more easily believe the lies he wants us to. We are more susceptible to the confusion he brings because our confidence is off-kilter, and it can convince us that we have no value or strength to fight back. The truth becomes skewed and lies are allowed to become our truth.

Spend a few moments thinking about any people you consider your enemies. What would it feel like to be in good standing with every person you know? That doesn't mean we all have to be friends, everyone is different, and that's okay. However, it means that if you ran into one of the people on your former "enemy" list, it wouldn't cause drama in your life. You could have a superficial chat and keep walking, rather than you wanting to hide or run in the other direction. In imagining your life without human enemies, can you see how good it would feel? With God's help, you can face the true enemy of your soul, the devil, forgive the people that have hurt you, and move forward in your healing process.

Exchange Old Locks for New Keys

Old Locks	New Keys
The enemy comes to steal or has stolen	I choose restorations: God restores and pay back *Genesis 50:20-21 The Message (MSG)*
The enemy comes to kill	I choose life: God brings back to life those things that were dead *Romans 4:17 (NIV)*
The enemy comes to destroy	I allow God to rebuild: God rebuilds in us the things he intended for us to have from the beginning *1 Peter 5:10-11 The Message (MSG)*

Moment with God

God, I don't know where to start, but I am deciding to trust that you do. If there are lies that I believe, please point those out to me and help me let go of them. Give me the courage to embrace the truth. I need you, Lord, to defeat the enemy of my life. Where important things have been stolen from my life, please help me to feel paid back. Where I have felt as though I would die from pain or hardship, please come and bring me a new life. Where I have almost been destroyed, please rebuild my heart to fullness. Help me to overcome fear with faith, and to believe all your promises. To know that when you make them, you keep them. Please bring me to a place free of fear.

Forgiveness

for·give /fərˈgiv/ verb
stop feeling angry or resentful toward (someone) for an offense, flaw, or mistake. Cancel (a debt). Synonyms: pardon, excuse, exonerate, absolve, acquit, let off, grant amnesty to.

I can remember a day when I considered "forgive" to be a four-letter word. Anger, hurt, and resentment reared up every time I thought of forgiving the person who violated me. Who would want to forgive someone who left lifelong scars? We are human, and with that comes a desire to take revenge. Thankfully, our loving father does not want us to take revenge. If He had set it up that way, the world would be in a worse state than it already is.

Never pay back evil with more evil. Do things in such a way that everyone can see you are honorable. Do all that you can to live in peace with everyone.

Romans 12:17-18 (NLT)

VERY IMPORTANT: Forgiveness does not diminish the impact of anything that has happened to you. It does not make the abuse you suffered okay. Imprisonment for a crime is a consequence. Forgiveness does not negate the consequences of actions. BUT GOD and the authorities He has appointed are the ones responsible for delivering those consequences, not us. When we forgive, we allow God to be the one who gets justice for us. Choosing forgiveness also frees us to move on and experience real joy. Then we can trust God more fully each time we forgive!

There is a difference between forgiveness and reconciliation. Forgiveness is a command in the Bible. God forgave us through Jesus, and He expects us to forgive each other no matter what the offense. Forgiveness happens on the inside, but reconciliation is on the outside. When you forgive, you do not have to expect to reconcile the relationship. It's possible, but not required. Without it, you can still experience all the benefits of forgiveness. At first, I thought that forgiveness meant that I would now have to be in a relationship with my abuser. No, thank you. However, letting go of what your abuser did to you and not wanting revenge is part of forgiveness. When you can think of that person and no longer hope that something as bad as what they did to you, will happen to them, you will experience great peace!

When I first faced my past, I had zero desire to forgive. Truthfully, I don't think I ever really understood what forgiveness meant. I realized that I had to go through everything I've shared in the earlier chapters first. I had to understand and give myself the freedom to feel and make choices based on what I needed. Mourning what I had lost helped me move past the sorrow and begin to accept my overall feelings. Facing and understanding my anger prevented me from hurting others and motivated me to make changes and to include God. Once I learned who my true enemy was, I was able to start opening my heart and mind to the meaning of forgiveness. That put me on the road to being able to forgive.

In the next few paragraphs, you'll read about the main areas I needed to find forgiveness. I needed to forgive God, bystanders, and ultimately the person that abused me. Under each of the headings, there may have been a long list of hurts that kept me prisoner. Finding the keys for each of these took some time, but by identifying who I needed to forgive, it helped me sort out my feelings.

I Needed to Forgive God

I never really thought I blamed God, but I believed that God had a vendetta against me. I thought He held something against me from the beginning of my days and that, instead of taking me out with lightning, He let the abuse happen. As a child, I accepted Jesus out of fear. The people in my life said that I would "burn in a lake of fire" if I did not ask Him into my heart to save me from hell. So, this was how I saw God – with a significant amount of fear.

When we lived in the Seattle area, our pastors regularly said that God was a good God. It took a long time for me to believe this. After hearing this, my thought was, "well, maybe He is good to you," but then there is my story. Or, "I must know Him differently than you do." A few years after we were there, I was attending Pastor Gini's ladies' Bible study on a Tuesday morning. She repeated that God was a good God, louder and more clearly than I had ever heard it. It was like God himself was speaking right to me, and it bore straight into my soul (mind, will, and my emotions). "Ladies, our God is good ALL THE TIME, He is ONLY GOOD and CANNOT BE ANY LESS – HE NEVER CHANGES, and HE RELENTLESSLY PURSUES YOU WITH HIS GOODNESS." Wow, I was awake after that, although I heard nothing else that day at Bible study, as my mind had those words on re-play. I remember bowing my head, closing my eyes as if no one else was around and praying, "God, if you are that good, I want all that you have for me. Even if it seems strange, weird, or even completely crazy, I want all you have for me. Help me to accept what you have with a great attitude. In Jesus Name, Amen."

Can you see that what I held against God was nothing more than religion (traditions made up by people), not relationship (what we have through Jesus)? Although I was an adult, I was relying on information that I had learned in preschool! If God's priority is love and He is good (which I encourage you to choose to believe as I did), then that is where our focus can be as well.

You Need to Forgive God

Maybe like me, you may not realize that you have misunderstandings about who God is. The act of forgiving God isn't for Him; it's for you. Whether or not we realize it, we blame God and hold Him responsible for things that people do to us. Spend time thinking about whether you hold God responsible for the abuse you suffered, it's worthwhile. When we don't forgive God, it keeps Him at a distance and prevents us from receiving His help. When we forgive God, He can then help us because we are willing to accept it. Have you sought out groups that you could attend that will help you hear the truth? Try putting yourself in a place that will help you realize the truth about how much God loves you.

If this is too hard to consider, that's okay – remember every one of us is unique. We all do things in a different order and are ready for growth in different areas at different times. If you aren't ready to forgive God yet, I encourage you to tuck this away for later. However, the longer you wait to forgive God, the longer it will be before you can fully accept His help.

I Needed to Forgive Bystanders

I grew up attending church, and at the same time, was abused at home. No one knew. No one rescued me. Yet my father was a leader at our church. He was a deacon and the church pianist. But no one knew him, not really.

When people heard about my abuse, some did not believe me. My father had them all fooled. They questioned the authenticity of my story. The shock and judgment were almost as bad as the abuse. Over the years, I have told people what happened to me. Some were not mature enough to handle the information. Their responses often left another scar. People can be cruel.

If instead of forgiving these people along the way I chose to gather up all the offenses, I would not be strong enough to carry the weight. I am only five feet four inches tall as it is but adding the weight of those offenses would make me so much shorter!

Forgive Your Bystanders

For anyone who has experienced abuse, there are people that we feel "should have done something to save me." Whether it's our parents, teachers, or caretakers, we can easily hold on to unforgiveness towards these people. It is better to forgive bystanders for being human than holding a grudge and having it affect you. It Is to your great benefit to forgive them. You don't even have to tell them – you can tell God and let it go.

Maybe you'd like to know how to do this? It does seem like it should be some complex process. I found it was a decision and that once I made the decision, over time, my feelings followed. People will always let you down. That is something concrete in this world because of our humanity. You've let people down, too. Maybe you weren't there for them. The bystanders in your life may have been wrong not to have saved you but forgiving them will free you from what is still a connection between you and the abuse you suffered.

Questions to think about:

- Who are the bystanders in your life?
- Are you still in a relationship with them?
- Have you forgiven them for not saving you?
- Are there other people who have held responsible for what happened to you?

If you have identified anyone, write their name down. Now, rip up the paper into tiny pieces, and each time you rip say, "I forgive you." If you have the opportunity and desire to tell them in person, that works in addition to this exercise.

I Had to Forgive My Perpetrator

One of the first conversations I had in counseling was being told that sometime in the future, I would need to forgive my abuser. I laughed...out loud (an actual lol!) How could I? Honestly, I thought my counselor was the one who needed counseling. At that point, my focus was on how I'd get my revenge, forget about forgiveness. However, sometime after that conversation, I let go of thoughts of revenge and learned what forgiveness meant. It wasn't an overnight change; it took years until I learned that forgiveness was going to speed my journey toward healing. It motivated me to start the process. The process was tough, and I went through it – I held on tight to a thick layer of hurt. Forgiving took time. It was like peeling the layers of an onion, and there were a lot of tears. As soon as I would forgive one instance, pulling that layer off often revealed a lot more. It got easier each time, and I let go and forgave. Plus, I saw the benefit and felt lighter every time a layer disappeared.

Starting this process was overwhelming. I had so much to forgive. I did not even know where to start. My hurt was like a pile of unwearable clothing that, instead of getting rid of it, I would keep moving it from one place to another. This collection of hurts was so large and daunting that examining one piece at a time seemed impossible. To start chipping away at my "pile" of hurt, I needed God to intervene. I asked Him to help and open my heart and mind so that He could point out where to start. Some of it I did on my own with the Lord, and in some cases, I had friends, pastors and counselors who walked alongside me.

Have You Forgiven Your Perpetrator?

Forgiving the person who abused you is hard. As I said before, I would forgive one thing, and it would bring up ten more offenses. It hurts to face these things over again, BUT GOD (He interrupts our ways to bring His good ways) – as soon as we offer up those things and choose to forgive, He takes them for us. There may be days it'll be an effort for you not to pick them back up, but I urge you to decide in advance not to do that. Holding on to the anger you feel toward the person who hurt you keeps you chained to them. But when we choose to forgive, it breaks those chains. Have a simple talk with Jesus, as if you are having coffee with a friend. He will help you – ask Him. What would it feel like to have a complete release from being a captive to your past? Can you value yourself MORE than holding on to unforgiveness? Will you give yourself the gift of freedom and peace received through forgiveness?

I Needed to Forgive Myself

Because of the way I grew up, I watched a lot of television. It always made me wish I was in one of those TV families. The parents seemed to be perfect and always available for their kids. I had to learn a lot on my own, and when I had a question, it felt like I didn't have anyone to ask. As I got older, I ventured into a lot of things without much information. Because of this, I made a lot of mistakes and learned things the hard way. It doesn't absolve me of responsibility, but the way I learned resulted in a lot more mistakes and their consequences. Regretfully, I hurt people, and that regret kept me a prisoner, and kept me from forgiving myself. For me, forgiving myself was the hardest part. Maybe that sounds strange to you. I hope that you have more forgiveness for yourself than I had for myself. However, I think we are all too hard on ourselves. Our history repeats itself until we take responsibility for our actions. I had to be honest with myself. To forgive myself, I had to face things I had done wrong. Once I admitted these mistakes, I also had to let go of each one. Amazingly, the next time I faced a similar chance to screw up, it was easier to make the right choice. The process of facing my mistakes and forgiving myself gave me the power to make better decisions. Remember that you need to learn this skill – because we are human, we can count on making mistakes and dumb decisions. Forgiving yourself should become a habit, not a one-time occurrence. Make it a lifestyle.

How to Unlock Forgiveness

Where do you start? How do we sort it all out? One great place to start is to write down everything that you can think of that has hurt you. Everything that you hold on to even if it doesn't appear to have anything to do with your abuse.

Here's what it might look like:

God, where were you? Why didn't you send help? Why did you let evil into this world? I hate my abuser, my bystanders, and on some days, I even hate myself. How could people have been there and not done something to save me? Where were all my friends? Where was my family? What is wrong with me that I'm the one they choose to hurt? How could they have done that to me? It's all their fault. They left me just like everyone else always has. I can't connect with people; they do not understand me. Everyone else's lives are so much better than mine. Why does God let me have such a terrible life when all around me, people have such great lives? I can't even stand anyone around me right now. How could he/she treat me like I was nothing, like a slave, like an unimportant, useless thing to be used? I'm a terrible person. I have done so many wrong things. I can't forgive myself.

Can you see how this is a form of "word vomit"? A stream of thoughts thrown onto paper. Write yours out then read it – out loud. Listen to the words, listen to the hurt they hold, and how they keep you a slave. Breathe – take a deep breath. Close everything else out of your mind, shut-off your phone, and silence other thoughts for a couple of minutes, except for this – ask God to come. Ask Him to meet you where you are (He is speaking, you need to listen). Show Him what you wrote and tell Him you can't do it on your own because that is the truth – you can't, but He can. Ask for help to release it to Him and really mean it. We need to make a conscious effort to let God help us. BUT GOD - He is a good God who loves you more than you could ever imagine or hope for – He will come, He will rescue and help you.

Don't bargain with God. Be direct. Ask for what you need. This isn't a cat-and-mouse, hide-and-seek game we're in. If your child asks for bread, do you trick him with sawdust? If he asks for fish, do you scare him with a live snake on his plate? As bad as you are, you wouldn't think of such a thing. You're at least decent to your own children. So, don't you think the God who conceived you in love will be even better?

Matthew 7:7-11 The Message (MSG)

Forgiveness Can Get Confusing

There is a verse in the Bible that I once had the hardest time understanding:

If you forgive those who sin against you, your heavenly Father will forgive you."

Matthew 6:14 New Living Translation (NLT)

I got hung up on my thoughts about unforgiveness and had an internal dialogue with myself: If I haven't forgiven everything, is God up there holding a grudge against me? What if I'm unaware of things that I still need to forgive?

Here's what that verse means: If we have asked Jesus to come into our hearts, then we have forgiveness through Him. When we sin, it does not keep us from getting to heaven someday. However, when we hold on to unforgiveness against someone, it can block God's ability to work in us and through us. It keeps us captive to what the person did to us. We don't lose our ticket to heaven, but we lose the opportunity for freedom and joy in this life. God doesn't hold grudges.

Forgiveness is Equal Opportunity

Forgiveness. We all need to receive it, and we need to give it as well. No one is perfect in this world – we all screw up. Here is an account of a woman in the Bible who received forgiveness in a public setting from Jesus.

Jesus went across to Mount Olives, but he was soon back in the Temple again. Swarms of people came to him. He sat down and taught them. The religion scholars and Pharisees led in a woman who had been caught in an act of adultery. They stood her in plain sight of everyone and said, "Teacher, this woman was caught red-handed in the act of adultery. Moses, in the Law, gives orders to stone such persons. What do you say?" They were trying to trap him into saying something incriminating so they could bring charges against him. Jesus bent down and wrote with his finger in the dirt. They kept at him, badgering him. He straightened up and said, "The sinless one among you, go first: Throw the stone." Bending down again, he wrote some more in the dirt. Hearing that, they walked away, one after another, beginning with the oldest. The woman was left alone. Jesus stood up and spoke to her. "Woman, where are they? Does no one condemn you?" No one, Master." "Neither do I," said Jesus. "Go on your way. From now on, don't sin."

John 8:1-11 The Message (MSG)

Wow! What an incredible picture of how forgiveness works. We cannot point at others because, without Jesus, we are just as flawed as the next person! What a relief! Jesus doesn't expect us to be perfect, and so we, too, should not expect perfection in ourselves or others. We need His forgiveness, we need to forgive others, and we need to forgive ourselves.

How to Forgive

How can you forgive all that has happened to you? I know it is not easy. Here's how: take one act of forgiveness at a time. Each time something comes up from your past or present, decide to forgive. We all want and need people that love us, and for that to happen, we must learn to be forgiving. Accepting people for who they are, faults included, requires us to learn how to forgive regularly. Once you forgive what has happened in your past, you will find that it is easier to forgive anything that happens in your future.

Forgiveness is Worth the Effort

Forgiveness is letting go – for good. Forgiveness is for you. Jesus gave us forgiveness by giving His life for us. He forgave us, knowing that we would still sin. Through forgiveness, we receive a release from the cage built by abuse. When we forgive, we open the door to the cage so that God can come and help us. When we can make forgiveness a lifestyle, we can climb out of that cage and walk freely.

Martin Luther King, Jr said, *"Darkness cannot drive out darkness; only light can do that. Hate cannot drive out hate; only love can do that."* He also said, *"We must develop and maintain the capacity to forgive. He who is devoid of the power to forgive is devoid of the power to love. There is some good in the worst of us and some evil in the best of us. When we discover this, we are less prone to hate our enemies."*

Nelson Mandela spent 27 years in prison because he was taking a stand against apartheid. He said this of forgiveness, *"When a deep injury is done to us, we never heal until we forgive."*

Forgiveness is both an action and a feeling. We need to choose to forgive, and then the feelings will follow. It may take time for our emotions to catch up – they like to linger. It will take discipline. Practice makes perfect, by adopting a lifestyle of forgiveness, you will add the keys to peace and joy to your life!

Exchange Old Locks for New Keys

Old Locks	New Keys
Blaming God	I choose to forgive God *Colossians 3:13-14 The Message (MSG)*
Blaming bystanders	I choose to forgive bystanders *Matthew 6:14 (NLT)*
Blaming myself	I choose to forgive myself *Psalm 30:2-3 The Message (MSG)*

Moment with God

Dear God, please help me to forgive you. I forgive you for all the hurt in my past. I no longer hold any of it against you. I choose to let go of those things and believe that you are a good God who loves me. Help me to forgive the people around me that did not rescue me and to forgive the bystanders in my life. I choose to forgive them. I know I need to forgive the person(s) that abused me – help me, God. Please also help me to forgive myself, I am human, and I make mistakes, but I know that you can bring me peace and joy! In Jesus' name, Amen.

Perspective

per·spec·tive /pərˈspektiv/ noun
the state of one's ideas, the facts known to one, etc., in having a meaningful interrelationship.

My definition
how we look at the facets of our life based on the thought filters we operate with.

In this chapter, we are going to trade old locks that I call *faulty filters* in our minds. Then we'll learn how we can replace them with new keys, what I call *flourishing filters*, to right thinking. Each day we fill our minds with information. We process this information in infinite ways depending on our thought filters (what the information you receive is filtered through); we can see outcomes as positive, negative, with apathy, with anger, in any number of ways. Just like a paper coffee filter allows only the coffee through and not the grounds, to create a delicious hot beverage. Our thoughts with added filters can change the way we view and react to everyday situations in our lives. For example, if fear is your first filter, then hearing that someone was in a car accident can make you afraid that you will also get into a car accident.

I believe there are faulty filters and flourishing filters. We don't always choose what filters we are utilizing for our thoughts. We may not even realize that we have these filters that affect our thoughts and behaviors. They work like a lining over our mind an impact how we evaluate external circumstances. These filters, whether faulty or flourishing, change the way we see the world.

When you were abused, it taught you that people in general are not to be trusted. From then on, you probably have "lack of trust" as a faulty filter. This filter leaves us unable to attach to people because we don't trust them. Without trust, our relationships are a struggle. And, if we can never fully trust God with everything we are and have, it is difficult to rely on God as well all need to.

On the other hand, is a flourishing filter. I have known a few people that were taught by their parents that everyone loves them. To clarify further, everywhere they go, they never doubt, compare themselves, or worry about people liking them because their thought filter tells them "everyone loves me." For me, this blows my mind! What an amazing way to live, I still pray that I can believe that everyone loves me.

I hope you discover areas where your thought filters need to change so that you are more easily able to receive God's perspective. We often believe things that aren't true without giving it too much thought. Those beliefs can become our filters.

I have said this before, but we are all so different. The filters in my mind will differ in some ways from yours. So, as I share what I had to face, I suggest that you write down what thought filters you need to change. Take a moment and ask God to help you.

I Needed Discipline for My Mind

Throughout my life, I have had moments where, suddenly, on a typical day, memories of my abuse invaded my present. It used to stop me in my tracks. Our minds are incredible, aren't they? Whenever this has happened to me, it was like the memories physically pulled me back to the moment of abuse. I became locked in that moment as a victim. After I faced my memory, I would find myself angry and depressed. My past was still affecting and invading my present! "I have forgiven this, why is it coming up again," I would ask myself. And then I would add, "Help me, Jesus," often said out loud while gritting my teeth. To get over the anger, I had to forgive all over again, which is an exhausting process. To gain the perspective I needed, I had to choose in each moment to be angry but forgive the past. I had to remind myself of my present state so that I could set my mind on the future I wanted.

Yoga is a little too quiet for me. However, I do see its value and take a class every so often. They have some interesting things they say, most not really for me, but one stood out. The instructor mentioned having a "mantra." The first time I heard it, I didn't know what it meant, so I looked it up. *Mantra - an often-repeated word, formula, or phrase, often a truism.* That made me think, "I need a new mantra." I need new, repeated words that I am telling myself over and over to change my perspective and my thought filters.

Anytime I need to change the way I'm thinking, the only absolute truth that I have is the Bible. Because I believe that every Word in there is from God, and I know that He loves me, His Words are the ones I want to repeat to myself. I needed to add new keys from the Bible to help keep my past from invading my present. I created my own "mantra" of sorts; I found new words to tell myself over and over. As well as the truth of the Bible, I reminded myself of this as well: "I a no longer a victim. The truth is that God loves me and because of that, I can overcome the effects of my past. With God helping me, I am lovable, and I have an incredible future in front of me." I renewed my mind with better thinking by telling myself the truth, even if I did not believe it yet! Each time a memory popped into my mind, I would remind myself of these keys from the Words I found in the Bible. It became my new filter.

Your Thought Life

The truth often eludes us when we keep running on the hamster wheel of life. It is miraculous when we take the time to identify our thoughts. By taking an inventory of all that you believe is right or wrong in your life, you can find clues to how you make decisions and how what you are thinking about may drive those decisions. Look at what motivates you and why you do the things you do. Is it anger? Is it fear? It does not matter what choices you've made in the past. Let it go, give it to Jesus and ask for wisdom and perspective to change your thinking for your future.

Take the time to ask yourself these questions and be okay with your answers:

- Do you ever have memories from your past invade your present?
- Do you blame other people or your past for the way your life currently is?
- Is blame driving your choices?

- Is assigning fault for things going wrong in your life, keeping you from taking responsibility and moving forward?

In our lives, we can easily become convinced that "this is just the way things are," which can make us tolerate wrong thinking and not overcome. You deserve to live well. Let the answers to these questions sink in deep and ask God to show you ways that you can think differently.

I Needed to Think Differently About My Value

We can have a tainted sense of who we are because of sexual abuse. I used to take any little comment that people made about me, even innocently, as negative because of my faulty filter. My collection of these comments backed up my belief that I lacked any value. On top of that, I took what were even good comments and twisted them up to be negative and put that into my belief system. It was a chaotic mess of jumbled chains. My actions were wrong because of my wrong thinking.

I placed more value on what other people thought about me than on what I thought about myself. I did not think much of myself. I thought that was humility. Taking no credit for my accomplishments, I regularly let people take credit for what I did. It took way too many years to discern the difference between being humble and allowing people to walk all over me like a carpet. Desiring humility is a good thing, but I needed to recognize my own value.

I decided to explore why I did not take credit for my accomplishments with a counselor. In doing so, I discovered a memory. When I was a girl in elementary school, another girl in my class accused me of "thinking I was so great," and loudly pointed it out for all my class to hear, "look at the way she flips her hair, she thinks she's so pretty." It was from that point on that I never wanted anyone to give me credit, point out my accomplishments in public, or cause me to stand out in any way. As I got older, I adopted this as "humility." But do you know what happened as well? I became bitter. Every time someone took credit for my accomplishments, it hurt, it stung, and I tucked it away. The pain ate at my soul from not getting credit, and it built up over time. Finally, I could not take it anymore; I went to Jesus with this issue. At the time, I was embarrassed to admit to anyone, even my husband, how confused I was. My beliefs and knowledge were all skewed.

I asked God for wisdom, and He gave it to me! At first, He showed me that it was okay to take credit for my accomplishments, so I started there. Then He reminded me that I needed to care more about pleasing Him than pleasing people; this helped with the carpet like behavior. Understanding these points helped sort out my thoughts so that I could learn that I don't always need credit to have personal value. Little by little, I listened. He talked, I obeyed, and I gained the wisdom I needed for each step. I let go of the bitterness I had built up.

Because of my background, I easily misunderstood the truth and believed the lie that I was not worthy of receiving praise for my accomplishments. I needed God to break the lock of that lie so that I could be free to accept my value. Seeing my value is something I still struggle with; I have to work at being comfortable with my accomplishments. I have learned to say, "thank you," graciously. Inside I have to remind myself that it's okay to take credit for things that I have worked hard for and that God has enabled me to do.

Here is I tell myself now about humility (the definitions I've created and adopted):

Humility isn't being a carpet that people walk on; Humility is not pushing always to be first. Humility isn't belittling those below us and disrespecting those above us; Humility is accepting our place, whether it's high or low with respect and honor. Humility isn't always having to be the center of attention; Humility is graciously accepting with appreciation the credit we deserve.

Do You Value Yourself?

Evaluating our worth is not something I often hear people talk about. In my opinion, people spend a lot of time doing work to prove they have value over spending time contemplating their worth. The truth is God values us whether we do anything or not. Why don't we treat ourselves the same way? The Bible is very clear that God values us. Believing our creator, the God of the universe values us, can make it easier for us to value ourselves. He values us so much that He sent His Son to die so that we could be in relationship with Him. I don't know anyone who has ever done that other than Him.

Some examples of ways to demonstrate that we value ourselves are; eating healthy, getting plenty of sleep and exercise, spending time with people you love and that love you back. When we take care of ourselves, we tell our soul that we value it. You have enormous value and need to believe that deep within yourself. No one can make you believe this; it is a choice. No one can convince you, not even God Himself. Despite what you have thought or felt in the past – the truth is that no one can be you – you are unique. Right now, in this time, in your city, on your street, at your place of work, in whatever community you are a part of – God placed you there for a specific purpose.

Here are some questions to get you started on evaluating your belief system:

- Have you ever had someone start a rumor about you that was not true?
- Did you ever have a boyfriend, girlfriend, fiancé, or a spouse that broke up with you and told you all the reasons why you were not "the one"?
- Have you had a business partner that has pointed out all your faults and none of your good qualities?
- Were there teachers in your history that gave you the impression that you would never amount to much?
- Did your parents encourage you or discourage you?

Do any of these questions strike a chord with you? If they don't, can you think of some others? It's amazing that even if the people in our lives don't speak something specific, we pick up beliefs about ourselves that are negative and impactful. We need to choose to believe the good things even though the bad things are often easier to believe.

Triggers I Faced

I have come a long way with Jesus from where I was. There are still songs, though, that have the power to bring me right back to the place and time of my abuse. With the help of God, I refuse to allow it to leave me debilitated. Our senses are powerful. All five of them can act as a mental time machine. Sight, smell, touch, taste and sound all activate triggers for us. These triggers can remind us of the abuse that has taken place in our lives. These have been difficult for me to overcome and required both professional and spiritual guidance.

Did you know that memories that include our senses are a sign that the memory is real? In my circumstance, because I had repressed memories, this was an incredible tool. My triggers helped validate the truth of my memories. As hard as this was, I needed that validation to make me face what had happened and move forward.

I am in any way, saying that facing triggers is always helpful. Still, when I see childhood pictures of myself, I am pulled right back by what feels like an uncontrollable force. However, this is a lie of the enemy. With the help of counseling over the years, I have identified these triggers and have gained ways to overcome that that work for my personality. And, I still have to give these situations to Jesus.

What are Triggers you face?

Every day we are subjected to people saying things to us or about us that can hurt. Some of those instances aren't even intentional. You may need to identify words or actions that you've misunderstood because they trigger something in you from your past. Maybe there was something that happened recently, a small thing that you just cannot let go of? If so, it may be a sign that you have a trigger that has to do with some other experience in your life. A good counselor and Jesus can help you identify those connections.

Spend a few moments and include God in your thoughts and ask him to sort out where you have held on to things people have said about you. You can also talk to a counselor about triggers and get some tools to overcome those things in your life. Sit for a moment, be still, be quiet, take a deep breath, and allow yourself to rest.

Think about these questions:

- Do you have sights that trigger memories from your abuse?
- Do you have certain smells that trigger memories from your abuse?

- Do you have certain touches that trigger memories from your abuse?
- Do you have sounds that trigger memories from your abuse?
- Do you have certain tastes that trigger memories from your abuse?

Hurt in our lives, when not cared for, can leave gaping wounds that open us to reinjury. Jesus wants to come and heal those wounds. His love brings healing and strength. Have you ever noticed that the skin that grows where there was a cut is thicker and stronger? Once we allow Jesus to cover over our gaping wounds, there might be a scar there, but we need to look at that scar and realize we are stronger, and that no more hurt can get inside when we let Jesus fill that gap. We are stronger with Jesus!

This is what God wants for your life:

Are you tired? Worn out? Burned out on religion? Come to me. Getaway with me and you'll recover your life. I'll show you how to take a real rest. Walk with me and work with me—watch how I do it. Learn the unforced rhythms of grace. I won't lay anything heavy or ill-fitting on you. Keep company with me, and you'll learn to live freely and lightly.

Matthew 11:28-30 The Message (MSG)

I Needed to Know God's Voice

God's voice can get muffled and buried under all the other voices in our heads. His voice is the one we need the most. I used to find it very difficult to discern which voice was which. It kept me a slave to old things that had been said about me that turned into beliefs in my life.

When I was in high school, I took a typing class (yes, this was before there were computers in schools). My teacher was training people in this class to go into business. I was trying to avoid being in other courses and thought I might as well learn a skill that I could hopefully use. This teacher did not like me one bit. To this day, I don't know what I did that made her dislike me so much. Towards the end of the year, she told me straight out, "You will never make it in business, and I have no idea why you took my class." I was shocked. Honestly, I do not even remember what grade I got in her class, but what she said hit me like a ton of bricks. Thankfully I did not carry it for long. After graduation, I needed a full-time job. Despite my former teacher's comment, I got my first job because I could type. God used that first job to position me to work at a Christian Radio Program, where I met people who encouraged me in my faith. Can you see how a comment from one person could have set me on the wrong path? If I had held onto it, I would've thought, "I can't take that job because I can't type well."

It wasn't always easy for me to tell the difference between what God was saying and what the other voices in my head were saying. My own dysfunctional voice, my parents' voices, my teachers' voices, some of my leaders' voices were the most common in my head, but how was I to discern the difference and learn to hear God's voice. He was never pushy; he never blamed me; he never brought hurt or the feeling that I had disappointed Him. God's voice was kind, encouraging, and brought relief. In the church, I expected to hear from Him and was listening, but I wanted and needed to hear from Him more than just on Sundays. Once I came to this realization that I wanted more of Him, I spent more time being quiet while I had my morning coffee. Instead of racing to get my Bible and read it like something on my to-do list, I just sat, sipped, and listened. As I did this, I began to hear His voice, and I learned to recognize it. By utilizing the key belief that God truly is good all the time, I was able to discern when it was God's voice more easily.

Whose Voices Are You Listening To?

If you've never taken a few moments to identify whose voices influence your life, now would be a great time to think it through. As you think about it, write down whose voice you listen to the most. It may not be a negative voice, but it is helpful to be aware of whose it is, and its impact. We can choose to stay prisoners to past voices, or we can listen to God's voice that will be a key leading to freedom from past abuse.

Answer these questions about the voices you listen to:

- Do you hear things someone used to say about you?
- Are you listening to your own voice?

- Are you sure that you tell yourself the truth?
- Is it your parents' voices that you listen to?
- Is it a person's voice that you can identify?
- Is it a teacher?
- Are you listening to God's voice?

It is an incredible gift to us when we can identify God's voice speaking! He will be saying ALL good things about you and to you. His voice comes with feelings of peace, rest, and especially love. He is such a good God that He wants to help us and encourage us. You can trust His voice, always.

Our minds are often full of recordings on auto-replay. Over and over, all day long, we make decisions based on what we've heard from different voices over our lifetime. If we don't gain awareness of whose voices we listen to, we can end up living in chaos. What drives you? What are your goals? Do money, power, or recognition motivate you? Often, whether we realize it or not, we are listening to someone. We tell ourselves lots of things all day as well. What are you telling yourself?

How do we know whose voice we're hearing? Is it our own crazy thoughts? Is it parental brainwashing? Is it God? Is it the devil? The devil is not able to speak as a voice in our head, but he is a great illusionist. He can influence your decisions by continuing to deceive you outwardly, but he is unable to talk directly into your mind.

God is love, His voice in your head is always going to line up with what the Bible says because those are His words. That does not mean He will always say what you want to hear. But His voice will be one of encouragement, one prompting you to do the right thing, one that will uplift, and one that will help your situation. He won't bring shame; He will give you hope. To help make sure it is God's voice, we need to spend time reading and hearing His Words. Being in a thriving church is a great place to start.

This verse from the Bible makes a great prayer:

Keep me from lying to myself; give me the privilege of knowing your instructions.

Psalm 119:29 New Living Translation (NLT)

What Strengthening Your Mind Will Do

We are all born needy. As infants, we cannot take care of ourselves. BUT GOD, with the help of flawed humans, has brought us to this point. However, our journey through life has the potential to leave us like an unfinished home. Our souls (our mind, will, and emotions) have empty places that we try to fill with useless pursuits. Unless we fill these holes with God's Living Word, we keep pursuing unfulfilling things. What's great about God is that He doesn't want to come in and tear down what we've built. Instead, He desires to help us remodel. All that it costs is our willingness to let go and allow Him to work. He will do the rest, and you'll become who He meant you to be! He wants to unlock those old rusty places in your heart, add some updates, and bring new shiny keys to your remodeled heart.

Keeping Your Mind Strong

One way that I strengthen my mind using the Bible is word studies. Meaning, I will take a word or phrase that I know will help me and look up verses that contain those words. You can use the Bible App or Bible Gateway website; there are many resources. I found that this gave me verses that applied to what I needed at that time (not all will necessarily apply to what you need at any given time).

I have also found devotionals written by some of my favorite Christian authors extremely helpful. Amazingly enough, taking the time each day to read these five-minute devotions, I have found the topics to be just what I needed each day. I am so thankful for faithful leaders that are willing to give their time and energy to encourage people.

The strength I gained filling up my mind with the Bible was sometimes hard to hold on to. When we face any hardship, it can drain us. I had to surrender my mind to God and ask Him to protect what He put in me. In asking this, I believe it reminded me how much I needed to lean on Him.

Changing Out Faulty Filters

Living in Texas hill country (the Austin area), either our heater or our air conditioning is running a large portion of the time. Our filter for this system, thanks to an overwhelming number of allergens in our beautiful area, turns black and has to be changed every month. We don't always notice if it's been over a month since we changed it thanks to full lives. However, when it is changed to a nice clean filter, we immediately can tell the difference. When it's fresh, it is like an example of a flourishing filter.

Our refrigerator water filter is the same. We have hard water that constantly makes use of the contents of the filter to clean our water. The light on our refrigerator will turn purple, signifying that soon we will need to change the filter. Just like the air filter, thanks to our wonderfully full lives, this light will ultimately turn red. Not too long after that, different from the air filter, we do notice our coffee tastes bitter and our ice cubes do as well. Once it's changed, this is like another example of a flourishing filter.

My favorite type of filters in our house are the coffee filters. They may not be able to change the taste of water, but what they do bring is my morning coffee. And those little paper filters do a fantastic job – that is why I love them! Each morning, or evening before if I remember, I set one of those sweet brown paper filters into the coffee machine and the add my just-ground favorite organic dark roasted coffee. Voila! A few minutes later – my favorite filters have done what they were supposed to do – make me incredibly happy and WAKE ME UP! I'm not necessarily a morning person – my people can attest to that. Daily when I add that fresh new brown paper filter, it is my favorite flourishing filter!

All these filters have good outcomes; fresh air, clean water, and delicious caffeinated beverage. But what if we never changed them? What if we let them stay dirty? We would be breathing everything that we are allergic to, drinking bitter water and I would waste my coffee beans because no one would drink that coffee. Filters are important; we need them.

How to Recognize God's Voice

When we hear God's voice, we can use these criteria to know that it is His and not someone else's. I want to encourage you to adapt these truths into your belief system. I use "if," "then." This is the way of life. If I work, I get a paycheck. If I put gas in my car, then it runs. These are "if," "then," statements that help us to know that we are hearing God's voice!

The Truth	If	Then	The Benefit for Me
God is love	If God is love...	Then feelings of shame won't follow His voice; feelings of love will	I gain His love in my life!
God creates life	If God brings life...	Then I will feel energized when I hear from Him	I gain His life-giving energy!
God gives peace	If God brings peace...	Then I will have a sense of calm when I hear His voice and not stress or chaos	I gain peace in my life!
God creates with order	If God brings order...	Then His worlds will bring order to my mind	I gain order for my days!
God gives joy	If God brings joy...	Then I can choose to accept joy no matter my circumstances	I gain joy in good times and bad!
God sent Jesus so that we are forgiven when we choose him	If Jesus brings forgiveness...	Then I can forgive others because I am forgiven	I gain forgiveness and freedom from my past!

An Unlikely Hero

I want to introduce you to a woman I've read about; her name is Rahab. Her exotic name fits her perfectly. She is physically beautiful with skin everyone wants and hair that waves as she walks by you. Her smile stops people in their tracks. Everyone wants to be her and know her. Rahab isn't just beautiful. She's smart. She's a planner who provides for all her family's needs. Rahab is connected; she knows all the right people and is up on all current events. She's also brave. When her family was in danger, she did what it took to make sure they stayed alive. When all the people in her city were about to be destroyed, Rahab used her connections to ensure the safety of her family. Rahab was a daughter, a sibling, a well-known woman in her community, a friend to her enemies – Rahab was also a prostitute.

As you first read the description of Rahab, did you envy her? Maybe you did. I have always loved Rahab. The courage she had to go against all the odds gives me hope. It has helped me to see that I can also be brave. Her strength to go beyond what people must have thought of her made me realize that it does not matter where I come from or what I have done; I can have a great life now.

The voices in our head can try to tell us we aren't good enough, especially compared to what we see in other people, like Rahab. However, we find out that her life hasn't been a bed of roses. She has had to sell her body to make ends meet. Regardless, God provides a way out of a terrible situation through her bravery, her smarts, and her connections. Rahab chooses to be brave, and she makes a deal with the people whose army is coming to destroy her city. No matter what her family or anyone else had ever said about Rahab and her choices, she saved her whole family. Her strength shines through and brings life instead of imminent doom for her mother, father, brothers, and sisters. Whatever they had thought about her – THAT ALL CHANGED! Rahab and her whole family were spared the day that death came and killed everyone else in her city.

To do what she did, Rahab had to let go of any preconceived thoughts she had. She had to keep going even if she was afraid. She had to act so that she and her family would live instead of die. What if instead, she had believed all the bad things everyone had said about her? As a prostitute, what qualifications did she have to save her family? Letting go of her past was essential to ensuring her future. In doing this, she saved many more than just herself. Rahab used her key to bravery, letting go of things people believed about her to prevent a death sentence.

It's not easy to let go of fear. But doing things even when we are afraid – that's bravery. Without fear, there is no need for courage. You are not alone – God, the Creator of Our Universe, wants to come and meet you right where you are just like He did for Rahab, a prostitute. It doesn't matter who you are, what people have said about you, what you believe about yourself, or even what you've done. He thinks only good thoughts about you. Choose to listen to what He is saying.

Exchange Old Locks for New Keys

Old Locks	New Keys
Cluttered mind with faulty filters	I have a disciplined mind with flourishing filters *Proverbs 15:32 The Message (MSG)*
Dramatically affected by triggers	I surrender my past and everything that brings it back to my mind to Jesus *Matthew 11:28-30 The Message (MSG)*
Voices in my head	I hear God's voice *Psalm 51:6 (NLT)*
Weak-minded	I am bold, strong, and very courageous *Joshua 1:9 (NKJV)*

Be Intentional

To help reset your thinking, I recommend that you spend a whole week praying just for yourself. Doing this will take discipline. For the entire week, each time you think about a need – ask God to help you with it. When you sit and drink your coffee, ask God who you are. While you are in the car on your way somewhere – ask Him to be the loudest voice speaking to you. Trust that He will have all good things to say. Be sure to listen.

Moment with God

God, please help me, my mind gets distracted, and I lose focus on what you want to do for me. Change my mind to think like you. Help me let go of things people have said about me in the past and grab hold of what you say about me. God, please make your voice the loudest in my head. I want to hear from you and make decisions based on your wisdom. Help me to see myself from your perspective and not the way I have perceived myself in the past. In Jesus' name, Amen.

Wisdom

wis·dom /ˈwizdəm/ noun
the quality of having experience, knowledge, and good judgment; the quality of being wise

Synonyms: sagacity, sageness, intelligence, understanding, insight, perception, perceptiveness, acuity, discernment, sense, good sense, common sense, shrewdness, astuteness, smartness, judiciousness, judgment, clear-sightedness, prudence

I define wisdom this way: listening to God's voice first in decision making; surrendering the belief that we know more than God in any given situation; choosing to listen and obey His voice over any other in our minds; understanding from God that goes beyond the knowledge we've gained and the abilities we've acquired

Often, we confuse knowledge, what we've learned, with wisdom. We start learning the minute we are born. As babies, when we cry, it indicates we need something and those caring for us respond. Around the age of one, we learn to walk and receive praise for it. Starting at a young age, we start academics. Our minds are designed for learning. Each new experience creates new neural pathways, and those that we use the most stay with us for life. Along the way, some of us learn that people are unsafe. Because we gain a view that people are unsafe, we develop coping mechanisms. The knowledge gained from circumstances beyond our control teaches us a lack of trust. Facing trauma shows us that there is a lot to be afraid of in this world. If we experience bullying, are teased or made fun of, we can carry that as false knowledge that we are not good enough. When we are abused, the same occurs. Abuse can cause us to think that we are not good enough. Knowledge can be positive, and knowledge can be negative.

Knowledge isn't wisdom. The knowledge that we have is made up of the information, skills and abilities we've learned. Wisdom is more encompassing than knowledge and can seem somewhat elusive. When we think of the word wisdom, different pictures pop into our heads. Maybe you see Gandalf from Lord of the Rings or President Abraham Lincoln (he's my favorite U.S. President). It's hard to get a picture of wisdom. Wisdom isn't just a gift given to you once you start growing gray hair. Wisdom comes from God.

I used to think wisdom was only found in much older people until I reached the age that my children thought I was old. I faced a four-year-old who considered me old when I was only thirty! Great perspective! And when she started to question my authority, I realized I'd better get "old" really quickly or ask for wisdom. My oldest was born, believing she's always right. At the age of four, she told me it was okay for her to dress however she wanted (wearing two prints, one with purple polka dots and one with orange paisley). She reasoned that "Jesus doesn't care what I wear, Mommy." How in the world was I supposed to argue with that! That was when I started praying for wisdom. I realized I'd better get some understanding beyond my abilities and knowledge!

In this chapter, we will learn the areas of our life where we especially need wisdom as a key to help us overcome our past. We will learn that having wise friends can help unlock wisdom in our own lives. When we behave with thoughtfulness, by purposefully acting based on wisdom, we can change our life for the better. After that, we'll investigate what we are allowing to influence us by what we choose to watch and read. My prayer is that by the end of this chapter, you will recognize some areas in your life that you may need to add wisdom to and see the potential benefit.

I Needed Wisdom for My Choices

I haven't always relied on God's wisdom to make choices. Many of my choices had negative consequences, not only in my life but also in the lives of other people. Broken relationships for one reason or another, overspending, overdrinking, overeating, over, and over, and over. I didn't do anything without being extreme about it. By the time I noticed, I was overweight, overspent, and overdone altogether! Without any thought of where God was in this, I tried to overcome what I had done by my own strength, to no avail. I am so thankful that God doesn't expect us to be perfect but continues to help us grow no matter our age or stage.

Finally, I asked God to help me. I sat in my room with my head in my hands, and I gave up. With nowhere left to turn, I heard Him say, "It's okay, your life isn't over. We can dig our way out of this hole together. One shovelful at a time. Here's the shovel." One step at a time, one shovelful, one more and another one – I got past the consequences of my choices. What's great is that God did not condemn me, He did not give up on me, and He did not allow me to give up on myself. He got right into that ditch with me and handed me a shovel. God comes to rescue us, but He doesn't do it all for us; He does it with us when we include Him. And, what's terrific about His help – he's nice about it! There were so many times that I made unwise choices, BUT GOD so graciously helped me overcome the consequences.

I am now so thankful that I learned my lessons in those times because later, when it came to more significant decisions, I chose wisely. The first important choice I faced was when I heard God tell me that I was supposed to marry my now-husband, Joel. I am so very thankful that I listened and obeyed. Had I not listened to God in that decision, I would not have my husband and our three amazing daughters. The second wise decision was listening and obeying God about joining The City Church in Kirkland, WA. We, in a spiritual sense, "grew up there." Another wise choice was moving to Austin, TX to help start Expression Church. It is here in Austin that we have truly seen glimpses of what God wants to do in us and through us. I'm so thankful that God taught me to lean on His wisdom and not my knowledge. When we practice wisdom in our small choices, we can utilize the key of wisdom to make better large choices.

How Do You Make Wise Choices?

Getting a new job, switching to another church, moving to another state are all life changes that can have significant consequences. If we don't seek God's help and confirm our choices with the wise counsel of God, friends, and family, life can take a turn for the worse when we choose wrongly. But, how do we evaluate and ensure that our choices are right? Making wise decisions can seem daunting.

On top of that, discerning God's voice when our emotions are involved, can make our choices more complicated. I don't believe we can do everything right all the time, we are human, and to be human is to be flawed. Accepting our flaws is part of life. However, if we are careful about our choices by asking for God's wisdom, we can get closer to the right decision each time, especially for those with life-altering outcomes. Choosing to respond to life with God's wisdom instead of reacting out of emotion can bring the key of peace into our lives. When we choose wisdom one of the benefits is peace! Here's what the Bible says about where we can focus our thoughts to help us gain wisdom:

> Summing it all up, friends, I'd say you'll do best by filling your minds and meditating on things true, noble, reputable, authentic, compelling, gracious—the best, not the worst; the beautiful, not the ugly; things to praise, not things to curse. Put into practice what you learned from me, what you heard and saw and realized. Do that, and God, who makes everything work together, will work you into his most excellent harmonies.

Philippians 4:8-9 The Message (MSG)

In these modern days, we have endless choices. Visit the cereal aisle in any US grocery store, and you will find yourself overwhelmed. Options are wonderful but can be too much to handle, especially if you are in a season when you are facing your past. We are bombarded with marketing messages everywhere we go. So, how do we make good choices? Simplify. We overcomplicate our lives. Ask yourself what you need to live your life. Shelter, Food & Water, Family, Transportation, Jesus...simplify everything and start choosing what is most important. Simplification unlocks time – an irreplaceable resource. Unlocking time frees us to focus on what is important in our lives.

Here are some questions to think about:

- Looking back on your life, can you see the choices you made from an emotional response?
- Was the outcome beneficial in your life?
- Have there been times when you have listened to wise counsel?

- What was the outcome at that time?

Take a few moments and allow yourself to be quiet (no phone, no distractions, no noise), and listen for God's voice of wisdom.

I Needed God's Wisdom in Family Relationships

When I was growing up in the Boston area, our Pastor's wife would say, "Everybody is somebody's crazy relative." I love this saying! It's so true, and I have often been classified as that crazy relative. I'm loud, we homeschooled our kids, and I'm always quoting the Bible. These are just a few of the many ways that I am different from my extended family. Truthfully, they don't care – they love me. But I cared, and I had preconceived ideas about who they were and what they thought of me, because of things that were said when I was a kid. Our brains can lie to us. We have to be careful not to keep old offenses that belong to someone else when it comes to extended family.

As I wrote about earlier, my Nana came to visit me in Seattle the year before she died. Growing up, I can remember conversations where she was touted as "crazy," often by the people in our family and extended family. No one was quiet about it, and she knew about it as well. During her visit to Seattle, my babies fell asleep in their car seats, so we sat with them in the car so as not to wake them. It was just the two of us (except for the sleeping babies, of course). She shared with me that she, too, had been sexually abused by her father, and no one had believed her. All those years, she suffered without help. Her mother had told her, that was, "just the way things are." At that moment with her, I apologized for everyone that had ever thought she was crazy. I was able to unlock and release her just by listening and believing her. We embraced across the center console, and I told her how much I loved her.

Thankfully, because of my background, I had immediate compassion when she shared that with me. But I did regret all the negative thoughts I had about her, caused by what others had said. With the weight of how important family is – we need wisdom. We need to ask God to help us in our family relationships. I never would've found out about her abuse if I had cut off the relationship with my Nana as other people did. How thankful I am that I got to see her the year before she died. We need to use God's wisdom as a key to sort out the truth.

You Need Wisdom for Your Family Relationships

In our families, there are difficult people; in fact, the people we know the best are often the most difficult! That is *because* we get to know them the best. When abuse happens, it affects everyone, even those indirectly involved. We need our families. They are a proving ground where we learn how to have lasting relationships. And they are our people whether we want them or not. They are the original people God gave us. We need God's wisdom to overcome the dysfunction that is so prevalent in our families. It is an attack of the enemy. When we utilize wisdom as a key in our family relationships, we can rise above the attitude of that's "just the way things are."

These are some questions to think about regarding family:

- Does anyone in your family live in denial (refusing to accept the truth about something that is happening or has happened)?
- When the truth comes out in any area, how is it handled?
- Do you feel like you are respected and loved in your family relationships?
- Have you experienced anyone in your family having overly emotional outbursts?

Taking time to understand how the answers to these questions affect your life is important. When we think about how these situations impacted our lives in the past, we can identify areas where we need wisdom for our family relationships for the future. Also, understanding our family dynamics can bring wisdom to our self-awareness. Our family relationships can affect every area of our lives.

I Needed God's Wisdom for Friendships

I love people. I get my energy from being with lots of people and thrive when I'm planning a party. A friend of mine often jokes and says that I'm not just an extrovert; she often calls me an "outrovert." It's true. I'm not afraid to talk to anyone and enjoy talking to people wherever I am. If you've ever been complimented on something you're wearing or your hairdo by a random person while out shopping – that might have been me. My thought is, if I can make someone's day by sharing a compliment, why not share it. We need more smiling in this world, and I want to be part of that!

Making friends has always come easily for me. I'm friendly and not easily offended, and I'm easy to please as well. I know now that it's my natural personality. But the flip side is that in the past, I have had friends who were not trustworthy, unkind, and were easily offended. I have exhausted myself trying to please people that were impossible to please! It has stolen precious time from taking care of myself and my family, it has stolen my belief in myself, and it has stolen time I could have spent with people who genuinely appreciate who I am.

Years ago, I read a book called "Enjoy Life" by Marilyn Hickey. It opened my eyes and helped me to start choosing my friends more wisely. I realized that I thought so little of myself that I was "just thankful I had friends." This belief was magnified by living far away from our family. I never felt as if I was important to anyone. Realizing I'd be happy with a few well-chosen friends made things so much better for me! Sorting this out took some time. I prayed and asked God for wisdom, choosing which friends to spend the most time with, and it changed the way I was able to enjoy my life. I didn't stop being friends with everyone I knew, BUT GOD gave me wisdom about who to spend time with and from whom I should take advice. Our friends have a significant influence on us and it can either enslave us or free us.

You Need Wisdom for Friendships

Friendship is a vital part of our lives. Having good friends around you can often make or break you. How do we choose them well? A good friend will tell you the truth. If you have spinach in your teeth (this happens to me a lot), you want a friend that will let you know before you go about your day with an ugly green leaf showing each time you smile. A good friend shows up when you need them, not necessarily in person, but in whatever capacity they are able. A good friend has faith to believe good things for you, and they believe the best about you. A good friend shares your values. A good friend will respect that you have your own opinions, even though you may disagree on things, whether politics, religion, or anything else.

Here is a list of questions to ask yourself about the relationships you currently have:

- After being with my friends, how do I feel, do I feel good or bad about myself?
- Am I influenced to make wise choices when I am with my friends or not?
- Do my friend's values that line up with mine?
- Do I avoid friends that tell me the truth?
- If you could choose the perfect friend, what qualities would they have?
- Do the friends you have now have these qualities?

We cannot expect our friends to be perfect but having key friends with many of the qualities we value is certainly attainable. Ask God for wisdom in discerning which of your friends you should let influence you. This is a key that unlocks wisdom in our lives.

I Needed Wisdom for Input

As I've walked this journey, I understand more and more how the effect of what I'm listening to, watching, and reading impacts me. Because of my past, I am more sensitive to what I take in. When I was a child, I was subjected to pornography regularly. It was readily available in our home. There are boundaries I have had to set on what kind of input I allow for myself. For instance, I have cut out rated R movies and am very careful even with PG-13 movies. Anytime that I have veered from this commitment, I regret it. By compromising what I know is wisdom for my life, the consequences are often nightmares and loss of sleep. I also walk away from conversations that are inappropriate for my sensitivities and there are places I am careful not to visit. A few years ago, I realized that I needed to be careful what wording I used when searching for anything on the internet. I need wisdom for all the input I allow.

In recent years, I attended what our church calls a "Team Restore" night. The goal of this night was to hear from God about the situations in my life. I met with three people for a couple of hours. They did not know ahead of time who was coming but had been praying for me in the weeks before my attendance. As they prepared, they heard from God that I needed more healing in my life.

As we met, they asked me to pray about my past with them. During that time, God pointed out that lust was a generational curse in my family, and that we needed to pray it off me. I had never thought that I had any responsibility in that area because I had been the victim, not the abuser. However, all day before that night with them, I had prayed and asked God to help me be ready for whatever I needed to address. When they asked me to pray for forgiveness, I was hurt, and I did not want to, because it meant I had to take ownership. What I did not realize or want to acknowledge was that, even though lust in my heart was encouraged by the abuse and the things I had seen, it was still there. As an adult, I now had to take ownership of lust to be able to give it up!! I prayed and asked God for forgiveness for any lust in my life and lust in my family's past generations. It was a truly miraculous moment. As soon as I asked for forgiveness, I felt a physical lifting of the weight of this sin. I had not realized how much it had weighed me down! It was like I had been wearing ten layers of football pads on my shoulders all these years, and now they had been removed. Ever since then, when I am tempted to look the wrong way at a half-naked man, God reminds me of that moment. When I dare to think less of who God created someone to be, the Holy Spirit reminds me of who that person is in His eyes. We all deserve to have people see us as God sees us. He knows us better than we know ourselves, and He wants to help us to be our best selves.

What a huge difference this kind of wise input in my life made, as opposed to all the other input I get daily. God's input in those hours with faithful people changed how I live! By paying close attention to what kind of input I am receiving, I know when God's voice is speaking. Having wisdom to filter my input changes my whole perspective.

You Need Wisdom for Input

It doesn't matter what you've chosen in the past, because there is nothing you can do to change that. BUT GOD can give you wisdom for your future! You can find the wisdom to unlock those things that have kept you prisoner, by picking up new keys to gain wisdom.

Whenever we focus our attention on an area of our lives, it can have the power to bring change. What we allow as input in our lives can bring life or death to our souls.

Spend some moments answering these questions:

- Have you thought about wisdom in your life concerning your input?
- What benefit do you get from the books, magazines, or internet articles that you read?
- What benefit do you get from television shows or movies that you watch (not that some can't be for entertainment value alone)?
- What benefit to you have in your life from the apps you use or from your smartphone?
- Do you play video games that affect your thoughts?
- Are you reading or watching pornographic material (anything with explicit sexual content)?
- Do you feel like you have used wisdom from God in your friendships, your actions, your decisions? What input are you allowing?
- What ways can you take action to add wisdom for the input in your life?

As you answer these questions, consider what changes to your input would be beneficial and ask God for wisdom.

Why Wisdom?

The pursuit of wisdom is not a new concept or long forgotten, but it takes attention and effort. God tells us to ask. William Shakespeare said, "The fool doth think he is wise, but the wise man knows himself to be a fool." Oprah Winfrey says this, "Turn your wounds into wisdom," and Eleanor Roosevelt said, "No one can make you feel inferior without your consent."

There was a man in ancient times named King Solomon. This king, King Solomon of Israel, would have a peak net worth today of $2.2 trillion. According to the Bible, he ruled from 970 BC to 931 BC, and during this time, he is said to have received 25 tons of gold for each of the 39 years of his reign. He was unimaginably wealthy. Here's what's incredible about his wealth – he never asked for it, he asked for wisdom. Check out what the Bible says:

That night God appeared to Solomon. God said, "What do you want from me? Ask." Solomon answered, "You were extravagantly generous with David, my father, and now you have made me king in his place. Establish, God, the words you spoke to my father, for you've given me a staggering task, ruling this mob of people. Yes, give me wisdom and knowledge as I come and go among this people—for who on his own is capable of leading these, your glorious people?" God answered Solomon, "This is what has come out of your heart: You didn't grasp for money, wealth, fame, and the doom of your enemies; you didn't even ask for a long life. You asked for wisdom and knowledge so you could govern well my people over whom I've made you king. Because of this, you get what you asked for—wisdom and knowledge. And I'm presenting you the rest as a bonus—money, wealth, and fame beyond anything the kings before or after you had or will have."

2 Chronicles 1:7-12 (NLT)

What an incredible conversation King Solomon had with God. He saw his position as king as a great responsibility instead of an opportunity to post to Facebook about his new role. He wasn't aiming to be "most popular," but he wanted to be a good king for the sake of his people. God saw his heart, and abundantly blessed him and his people for his humility.

Knowledge is excellent – it helps us tremendously. BUT GOD! His wisdom is what helps us use that knowledge to not only help ourselves but to help countless others. Let's decide to seek wisdom for every part of our lives. This is what you want:

God, teach me lessons for living so I can stay the course. Give me insight so I can do what you tell me — my whole life one long, obedient response. Guide me down the road of your commandments; I love traveling this freeway! Give me a bent for your words of wisdom, and not for piling up loot! Divert my eyes from toys and trinkets, invigorate me on the pilgrim way. Affirm your promises to me — promises made to all who fear you. Deflect the harsh words of my critics—but what you say is always so good. See how hungry I am for your counsel; preserve my life through your righteous ways!

Psalm 119:33-40 The Message (MSG)

Exchange Old Locks for New Keys

Old Locks	New Keys
Unwise friends	I choose to walk with the wise *Psalm 119-73-80 The Message (MSG)*
Unwise actions	I will act with thoughtfulness *James 3:13-16 The Message (MSG)*
Unwise input	I will use wisdom to filter what I am watching, reading, and listening to *Psalm 51-10 The Message (MSG)*
Unwise choices	I will make good choices that bring wisdom to my life *1 Corinthians 10:23-24 The Message (MSG)*

Moment with God

God, please give me wisdom above all. Help me to make wise decisions. Jesus, I need your wisdom for my friendships, help me to speak well, and be influenced by you. Thank you, Father, for helping me to make wise and careful choices for what I see, hear, and read so that my life glorifies you. Please give me the key to wisdom to unlock new perspectives and blessings in my life.

Identity

i·den·ti·ty /ˌīˈden(t)ədē/ noun - the characteristics determining who or what a person or thing is

My definition: our true selves considering God's love and how He sees us

Who Am I? How do we answer this question? How do I know who I am? Am I an academic, a jock, a beauty queen, a daughter, a sister, a store manager, or a hairdresser? Defining who we are can be elusive. How do we determine who we are? In our culture, everywhere we look, it appears that people know who they are. Social media platforms - YouTube, Instagram, TikTok, Snapchat, etc. all make it appear like everyone except for us has it together. But do they? The truth is that most of them are still trying to figure out who they are but are doing their best to show the world that they do. However, this does not negate the fact that we are affected by what we see.

Identity Defined

My youngest daughter plays volleyball. I regularly say that she won't run for any other reason except to get the ball (running is not her favorite). Volleyball is her sport, she owns it, and it shows in her enthusiasm on the court. She stays focused on where the ball is and what her coach is saying - nothing else.

Recently we had a conversation about her identity. I asked her directly, "who are you?" Blank stare. Finally, she answered, "I'm a volleyball player." Great start. I asked her what would happen if she got injured and never played volleyball again, then who would she be. Again, blank stare. At this point, she answered like most of us would, "I have no idea." Our conversation went on for a while longer, and we talked about who God made us to be, what our values are, and what we do to live out our values. We learned that even if we were to sit still somewhere, not doing anything, we would still be who we are. We are not what we do.

Finding out who we are, our identity, who God created us to be, is an incredible and worthy pursuit. Have you ever heard it said of someone, "they have gone out to find themselves?" I have heard people say this about a family member who is traveling to a far-off country trying to discover who they are. However, our identity can't be found in a foreign country. It's right within us. We need to ask God to show us, and He will. The pursuit to discover who we are is worth the effort. The benefits; confidence, truth, trust in ourselves and our abilities, the ability to set boundaries for ourselves and with others, etc. Discovering our identity is the key to living our lives the way God intended. We unlock true freedom to be ourselves.

I Had a Victim-Mindset

For most of my life, I lived with a victim-mindset. I faced circumstances, and people, thinking like I was still a victim. It was as if I still had to be a slave to every other person's bad choices. I lived trying to "get by" rather than being free to make my own choices and create the life I wanted. Fear ruled my choices, and the results were exhausting which caused me to give up. I viewed myself based on the way I thought others perceived me. Living with that old frame of mind made me think everyone was out to get me and that something bad could happen at any moment. Fear ruled my life.

I did not value myself. That victim-mindset also had a negative effect when people complimented me. Even though I would outwardly be grateful, my immediate inward response was to assume they were trying to manipulate me somehow. Then I would proceed to belittle their comments, mostly in my head, but sometimes out loud. Instead of receiving a compliment, I took it as a negative. That is part of the victim-mindset. I did not believe the things that were said, and I told myself the opposite. It resulted in a terrible and incorrect self-image. Self-care was always on the back burner – so far back that when others saw goodness in me, it had no impact on how I saw myself. I had myself locked into believing that I was not valuable.

Do You Have a Victim-Mindset?

Finding out whether or not you have a victim-mindset can be difficult. When you think one way and behave that way for so long, you become accustomed to and it seems normal. So, how do you start changing your thinking and realize that just because you were a victim – you no longer are?

Here are some questions to consider:

- Do you consider yourself valuable?
- Do you consider your opinions to be important?
- Do you treat yourself well?

If you have abuse in your past – you were a victim. That is past tense. Victim-mentality takes effort on your part to change. The abuse doesn't define you, although the effects linger. Despite what happened, you are still who God made you to be.

I Had a Bad Self-Image

When I was a child, people were always commenting on how pretty I was. However, this compliment ate away at my soul with every single word. My first thought when I heard this was that I didn't want to be seen as pretty because then maybe I would not have been attractive to my abuser. My second thought was of unbelief because thanks to the abuse I suffered, I felt ugly. I had myself locked into a low self-image.

In the spring of 1990, a movie came out called "Pretty Woman," with Julia Roberts and Richard Gere as the main characters. (disclaimer: I am not endorsing this movie but sharing a personal experience) Julia Roberts plays a prostitute that Richard Gere's character asks for directions from, and that is the beginning of what becomes a very complicated relationship. One scene of this movie has always stuck with me. Lying in bed, the two discuss how Julia Robert's character became a prostitute. In explaining how it happened, she finally replies to his questions, saying, "The bad things are easier to believe."

This statement rang true for me. Life is a struggle and often beats us up. We have to work to believe the good things, and in that, we have to believe that we are worth the work that it takes. I owned this thought, "the bad things are easier to believe." I adopted this into my belief system and became okay with believing the bad things.

How is Your Self Image?

Take an inventory of how you view yourself. We believe what we think and say! Because of this, we need to make sure that we are telling ourselves the truth. I believe all of the Bible is perfect truth, do you? When we choose truth and refuse to live in denial, it helps us see who we are from the right perspective. Also, by taking care of yourself physically – eating well and exercising, you tell your soul (your mind, will, and emotions), "I care about you." Then by deciding to believe what you tell yourself; your self-image can go from bad to good!

Having a healthy and positive self-image not only changes the way we see ourselves but how others view us as well. Spend some extra time this week exploring what your image of yourself truly is – honesty is the best policy if it represents the actual truth. Answer these questions for yourself:

- When you look in the mirror, who do you see?
- What do you tell yourself?
- Are the words you tell yourself kind?
- How can you improve what you are telling yourself?

Whatever you learn from these questions, ask God to help you see yourself as He sees you. He loves you and sees you as His precious child.

I Lacked Self-Control

The way I saw myself impacted the way I treated myself. I lacked self-control. I was in an ugly circle of poor eating habits, which made me tired and kept me from exercising. I felt that there was no hope and that I was powerless to break free. My lack of self-control also resulted in taking care of everyone else, instead of making time for the things I wanted to pursue. Self-control over the words that came out of my mouth was also a problem. I locked myself in an unhealthy spot because of a lack of self-control.

There have been times I've been asked to help in multiple areas (e.g., help in the kids' classes at church, act as Team Mom for my daughters' volleyball team, lead a table at Mothers Of Preschoolers - MOPS, etc.) so I would jump in. Then when it got tough to juggle – I would quit. Instead of relying on God's grace to help me through or asking for help, I caved into the pressure. Despite knowing that God had called me, I did not believe myself worthy of the calling, and I used this as an easy way out of difficulty. Holding on to the victim-mindset kept me a prisoner, unable to overcome my challenges with God's help. I locked myself into the belief that I was a quitter.

In addition to this, there were times I should have said "no" to help in activities. Because of my lack of self-confidence, I was afraid that if I refused, people would not like me. Fear kept me a slave to being overdone and exhausted. I needed self-control for my calendar. My lack of self-control kept me stuck in a cycle of overcommitting and quitting.

Having a victim-mindset, I also let other's control my life. I was unable to stick up for myself. There were many times that people took credit for my accomplishments, and I did not speak up. I let people volunteer me for jobs that I never agreed to, and I would show up and do the job anyway. In my marriage, there were many decisions made that I did not agree with, but I went along with them anyway. In letting other people control my life, it ate at my soul (my mind, will, and emotions). Because I lacked strength in my soul, I did not have the energy to stand up for myself. The ugly circle continued. I locked myself into believing that I could not have any control over my life.

There came a time when all the lack of self-control came together into the perfect storm. We still call it, "Theresa's very bad day." On this day, I said all the ugly things that came to my mind to whomever I was speaking. I chose not to do thing on my calendar as well as doing nothing that anyone wanted me to do. I quit. At the end of the day, I had to face the way the day had gone, not very well, not well at all, in fact.

I never wanted to be the person I was on that very bad day again. In response to the way I felt the next morning, I made changes. I asked myself this question, "if each day belonged to me (and technically being at home while my kids were little, I was my own boss) how would I expect myself to behave?" As a manager, ensuring that my employees take breaks throughout the day would be important to me. I would require all vacation days to be used up by the end of the year to promote a healthy work-life balance. In finding the answers to the question, a solution was found. By adding actual breaks in my days and planning space in my calendar for time with friends, I set a boundary and took back some control over my life. By setting these guidelines for myself (as my own boss), I adopted self-control in my life as a key to a more peaceful and happier me.

Do You Lack Self-Control?

Because of the ways abuse affects our thinking, it also affects our actions. Actions stem from what we are thinking about. Lack of self-control can result from what we have lost as a result of abuse. In what areas of your life do you lack self-control?

Self-Control does not only involve mastering over-indulgence: It helps us make good choices for our lives. It also includes owning our mistakes, and our weaknesses are another part. Self-Control enables us to say "no," to commitments; it involves standing up for your values. When you know what you value, then you can prioritize your time.

This exercise will point out to you what you need to explore further when it comes to finding areas of your life where you need more self-control. The key of self-control will set you free to be who you are meant to be. If at any point you do not easily know the answer, that's ok. I encourage you to write down the what you're thinking. There is amazing power in writing our thoughts down; the action repeating what we're thinking while writing it down, drives home the points to our brains. When you are finished, pray over what you've written, ask God to point out specific areas that you need to let Him come and help you change your mindset. Let Him unlock those things you thought about yourself that may be wrong. After that, add keys from the Bible to remind you of who you are.

Read over these questions to yourself out loud:

- Do you overindulge in areas that result in poor health?
- Do you make choices that leave time for you to take care of yourself?
- Can you stand your ground when challenged?
- Are you able to accept and believe compliments and praise?
- Do you take care of your soul (your mind, will & emotions)?
- Do you take care of your body (eating, sleeping, exercise)?
- Are you able to continue accomplish things despite hardship?
- Do you have opinions and stand by them even if they differ from those around you?
- Are there other areas where you have no self-control?

These questions are meant to help you identify areas where your self-control may have been affected by abuse. I highly recommend seeking counsel on how to have and improve self-control in your life. Self-control is an important skill that can help us become our best selves.

How I Identified Who I Am

When I was in high school, our Pastor loved having us take spiritual gifts tests and the Myers-Briggs personality test. Pastor Jim saw traits in me that I did not see in myself, and he used these tests to show those traits to me. He was great at pointing out all the positive things these tests revealed about how God made us. I remember some of the positive things I learned about myself. I am a natural helper, I love to teach, and I love people. The results of both the spiritual gifts test and the Myers-Briggs test affirmed these qualities.

Later, after facing much of my past, I went back to these tests as a starting point to find out who God made me. Along with those, I started focusing on what I valued. I spent some time exploring what other people value. I asked lots of questions of my friends and leaders. I also spent time learning what God values to help me narrow down my own. Once I knew what I valued, I set up the priorities in my life to reflect those values.

Discovering who I am was not an overnight process. I read books to explore personality types. I continued to ask other people about how they set their values. I learned that it was good to set my own even if mine were different.

The tools I used to help me figure out who I am were:
1. A spiritual gifts test like this one - **https://spiritualgiftstest.com/**
2. The Myers-Briggs Personality Test
3. Identifying my own values based on the Bible

When I first took the spiritual gifts test (in those days on a piece of paper that needed to be sent away for evaluation), it came back with the result that I am gifted at helping. What the test called "the gift of helps" was my most dominant gift. In school, this made so much sense – I was the first person to jump in when anyone needed help. I've never shied away from work. As a young adult, it was helpful to realize that there was more to my abilities. I began to see that there was a larger purpose to who I am, and that God was involved. God had blessed me with the willingness and capability to help wherever I could. Every so often, over the years since that time, I have taken the test again. I still have the gift of helps but now other gifts fit me better. It's been an incredible way to increase my self-awareness and develop a positive self-image.

The Myers-Briggs Personality Test revealed that I am the personality type ENTJ. That fits me perfectly! Here are my interpretations of what the test results mean – I am Extroverted – a lover of lots of time with people. I am Intuitive – street smart. I am Thinking – logical in the way I tend to think. And lastly, I am Judging – a supporter of the truth. Instead of looking at my loud, friendly behavior as as a negative trait like I did in the past, I now realize it helps me get to know people. Instead of thinking that I'm pushy about contacting people and letting them know I'm thinking of them, I realize that it's thoughtfulness! These are my very loose interpretations of what each term means and the way I help myself remember who I am. Please visit their website so that you can delve deeper into your personality type.

When I began the process of figuring out what I valued, it started with what irked me the most. As much as this may be a negative approach, it worked for me. I began evaluating conversations after I had them. After some conversations, I realized that I was left with feelings of loss and discouragement.

What I found was that these conversations lacked love. I knew that being loved, loving others and understanding God's love for me was something that, without it in my life, I would not be myself. I found that as I stepped back after a long conversation with a friend that what I hoped for the most was that they felt loved and that I felt the same as well. Love is the number one priority for me. It is my first core value.

In raising my girls, if I ever caught them lying, sneaking, or trying to deceive anyone in any way, I had to control my temper. The first time I defined for them that lying was not okay in our family, and would not be tolerated, I discovered my unbending, ungracious need for the truth. Tolerating any deception was out of the question. Because I loved my children, of course I did not want to destroy them each time there was a mistake – we are all human after all, and children are still learning. I stepped back and tried to figure out why it made me so overly angry. I discovered that I value the truth in my life so strongly because my life as a child was always one big lie. The outside world thought we were a perfect Christian family and we were not. This discovery helped me parent better instead of treating my girls as criminals. I unlocked that zeal for the truth is my second core value. Discovering this impacted not only my life but the life of my children as well.

How Do You Find Who You Are?

You need to know who you are at your core. This knowledge results in confidence and self-esteem. When you know who God made you, your life is full of purpose. Having a purpose in what we do each day, rather than just earning a paycheck, brings joy into everything we do. Even the most mundane tasks such as grocery shopping, doing laundry or washing dishes can gain great importance. We show off God's love to people when we live our lives to the fullest. Accepting Jesus into our lives and surrendering who we are to Him brings the fruits of the Holy Spirit: love, joy, peace, patience, kindness, gentleness, and self-control.

Spend a few moments considering these questions and take action if necessary:

- Can you see how these tools can help change your perspective?

- Have you ever taken a personality test?
- Do you know what you value?
- Are you aware that you have spiritual gifts that God has given you?
- Have you taken a spiritual gifts test?

Our true identity is found on the inside. It's related to our character and who God intends us to be.

> Because of this decision we don't evaluate people by what they have or how they look. We looked at the Messiah that way once and got it all wrong, as you know. We certainly don't look at him that way anymore. Now we look inside, and what we see is that anyone united with the Messiah gets a fresh start, is created new. The old life is gone; a new life burgeons! Look at it! All this comes from the God who settled the relationship between us and him, and then called us to settle our relationships with each other. God put the world square with himself through the Messiah, giving the world a fresh start by offering forgiveness of sins. God has given us the task of telling everyone what he is doing. We're Christ's representatives. God uses us to persuade men and women to drop their differences and enter into God's work of making things right between them. We're speaking for Christ himself now: Become friends with God; he's already a friend with you.

2 Corinthians 5:17-20 The Message (MSG)

Thinking Back

My daughter Anna was born prematurely. Weighing only four pounds, four ounces and twenty-one inches long, she was all skin and bones. Despite her size, Anna was strong physically, holding her head up on her own at a very early age. As a baby, she was a delight, content, and barely cried. Parenting her even when she was a busy toddler was a joy, and we hardly ever had to correct her. As she began her elementary school years, her personality became more and more evident. Her kindness, gentleness, patience and overall sweetness were clear.

If you asked me, I would love to take credit for who Anna is – but honestly, I can't. She is who she is because God put those things in her nature. I've lived with her, so I know she isn't perfect, but she has a natural congeniality that comes from God, not from me. There may be an argument for genes; I agree those are often a factor. However, my other two daughters are similar but not the same and their DNA is from the same two people. I was a nurturing mom, willing to drop work or daily chores for a card game, a hug, etc. However great a mom I may have been, I have been nowhere near perfect. I can only take credit for not hindering her nature but not what was naturally in her.

Take a few moments and think back to how you behaved as a child:

- Do you remember how you were as a child?
- Were you kind?
- Did you love animals?
- Were you the one on the playground starting up a game?
- Maybe you were the kid on the playground that made sure the rules were followed?
- What did you prefer to play with: dolls, Legos, balls, kitchen toys?
- Did you spend countless hours playing video games?
- When corrected, were you easily swayed to do the right thing?
- Would you consider yourself strong-willed or compliant as a child?

Make some notes about your natural traits and interests as a child. These notes can help you start sorting out who you truly are on the inside. Sometimes as adults, we forget. We forget what it was like to be on that playground just being a kid, naturally behaving the way we were meant to be. Encourage yourself to not look at negatively at who you were as a child. Dare to be proud of who you naturally are – this world needs more authentically confident people who are brave enough to be unique!

There are other clues as to who you truly are. Answering these questions as well will help you discern what that daily decisions you make say about who you are:

- What did I value in the past? (evident by my past choices)
- What do I value now? (evident by my current choices)
- What will I choose to value in the future? (what do I want to change)
- What were my priorities in the past? (evident by how I spent my time)
- What are my priorities now? (evident by how I spent my time)
- What will I choose to prioritize in the future? (when I look back in 10 years, how do I want to have spent my time)

Simple Simon

There is a person I remind myself of often when it comes to finding my true identity; his name was Simon. We will call him Simple Simon. Simple Simon lived in a small town. Simple Simon was a strong-bodied fisherman who knew his trade well. He owned a boat and nets. Simple Simon was not well-educated, and other than fishing didn't seem qualified for much else.

When Jesus came along, however, everything changed for Simple Simon. Jesus saw things in Simple Simon that were not so simplistic, and Jesus did not overlook those things in him. Jesus called Simon to follow Him and to become a member of His group. Then Jesus changed Simon's name to Peter! Simple Simon became Powerful Peter by answering the call to follow Jesus. Powerful Peter was *that* guy. The one who people listen to, the man who knew his opinion and was not afraid to share it. Powerful Peter walked on water! Powerful Peter spoke to hundreds of people, wrote multiple books, and traveled the world! Not only did he travel, but he did it in an era when traveling was incredibly life-threatening. From walking, to riding a donkey or camel, to going by boat, Peter traveled to share what God had done in his life. No matter what Simple Simon thought of himself, when Jesus came into his life, it brought out all those amazing qualities that were already in him. He became Powerful Peter with one conversation. In a moment, Simon became the Peter he was meant to be.

Can you see this for yourself? Can you imagine leaving everything in your life to follow Jesus? In a sense, when we choose Jesus, we can leave behind our past hurts and mistakes so that we can be who we were originally meant to be. We can choose to grab hold of His love, joy, peace, patience, kindness, gentleness, and self-control so that we can live full and amazing lives. We may not all be called to have the life that Peter had. But following Jesus will bring us to the wonderful life He has that is just right for us. What if by following Jesus, you gained a lifestyle of not waiting to do the "somedays" of your life, but you were able to move forward and make them happen? What if by following Jesus, you were able to have the restoration in your relationships that you have always wanted? If Simple Simon (a nobody from nowhere) can become Powerful Peter (a world-traveling author and speaker), then why can't you become who God created you to be?

Keep Learning

To help you discover who you are, I highly recommend that you decide that you always have more to learn. Have you ever met those people that answer, "I know" to everything you say? That is not the right attitude. We all have more to learn in every season. My kindergarten teacher was right, "Learn something new every day." By continuing to learn, it can put our perspective in the right space, too. By looking at our lives and choosing to learn new ways, increase understanding, and add to our knowledge, we become healthier, more well-rounded people.

Here's what the Bible says about the way we can live our lives:

> But what happens when we live God's way? He brings gifts into our lives, much the same way that fruit appears in an orchard—things like affection for others, exuberance about life, serenity. We develop a willingness to stick with things, a sense of compassion in the heart, and a conviction that a basic holiness permeates things and people. We find ourselves involved in loyal commitments, not needing to force our way in life, able to marshal and direct our energies wisely. Legalism is helpless in bringing this about; it only gets in the way. Among those who belong to Christ, everything connected with getting our

own way and mindlessly responding to what everyone else calls necessities is killed off for good—crucified.

Galatians 5:22-24 The Message (MSG)

But the Holy Spirit produces this kind of fruit in our lives: love, joy, peace, patience, kindness, goodness, faithfulness, gentleness, and self-control. There is no law against these things!

Galatians 5:22-23 New Living Translation (NLT)

Exchange Old Locks for New Keys

Old Locks	New Keys
Victim mentality	I choose a life free of the effects of what happened to me
	I choose to believe what God says which leads to joy *1 John 4:7-10 The Message (MSG)*
	I choose to trust God which brings peace *Philippians 4:6-7 The Message (MSG)*
Poor self-image and lack of self-care	I can believe the good things about myself
	I will make good choices that encourage my soul, body, and spirit
	I will ask God to help me see myself as He sees me and to treat myself with His kindness and gentleness
Lack of self-control – overindulgence, poor choices, not standing up for what I value	I will ask God to point out areas in my life where I need self-control
	I will ask God to help me make better choices
	I can stand up for what I value despite other people's opinions. I am unique and it's ok if my values and priorities differ from others

	Proverbs 16:32 New Living Translation (NLT)

Moment with God

Father help me to know who I am in you. Help me, God, to move forward from any victim-mentality that I have held on to. You love me, and I choose to believe that if the God of the Universe loves me, then I can love myself and accept love from others. I want self-control in my life, please show me what that looks like and help me to make good choices. In Jesus Name, Amen

Where Was God?

or·i·gin /ˈôrəjən/ noun
the first stage of existence; synonyms: beginning; ancestry, root, genesis, birth, lineage, creation

He Was with You in Your Origin Story

There you were, in your birth mother's womb. You were just a few cells combining and growing. God was there, too. He was making sure that you were created just as you were meant to be. Your DNA came together with all the information that makes you unique. And, He loved you before any other person ever saw you.

> Oh yes, you shaped me first inside, then out; you formed me in my mother's womb. I thank you, High God—you're breathtaking! Body and soul, I am marvelously made! I worship in adoration—what a creation! You know me inside and out, you know every bone in my body; You know exactly how I was made, bit by bit, how I was sculpted from nothing into something. Like an open book, you watched me grow from conception to birth; all the stages of my life were spread out before you, the days of my life all prepared before I'd even lived one day."

Psalm 139:13-16 The Message (MSG)

"If God is good, then why does He allow bad things to happen?" I would not be surprised if this is the most common question people ask about God's nature. I have asked this same question of Him, and I have had this very same question pointed at me from a family member regarding the Holocaust. Honestly, my family member had a good point. The Holocaust is a perfect example of evil in our world. It was horrific. Why would a loving God allow such painful things to happen to people?

For me, this question plagued me. I was abused as a small innocent child. Why didn't God protect me from that? Why didn't He send someone to prevent it? It's hard to admit, but the answer is a simple one. God gave us the gift of choosing how we would live our lives.

We All Have Choices

All over our world, people are constantly fighting for freedom. The freedom to choose who governs their land, the freedom to choose their religion, the freedom to smoke what they want, and so on. The list never ends of what people will fight for the freedom to participate in, say, and do. When God granted us the ability to choose our way of life, it opened this freedom to everyone. Unfortunately, the freedom to choose includes the good and the bad. Instead of being puppets, with Him as the puppeteer, God wanted us to be able to choose.

You see, God loves us. He loves us so much that He had no desire to put us on strings like Pinocchio. We were not meant to be puppets but to be living, breathing, thinking, decision-making, loving participants in this life. God did not want anything bad to happen in your life. His nature is always good, and therefore He would never choose abuse for you.

I Tried to See Him

Throughout my lifetime, I've tried to comprehend where God was while I was being abused. I was trying to picture Him from my limited human perspective. If God is omnipresent (able to be everywhere all the time), then Was He there idly standing by? How could He be a loving God? These thoughts, at times, held my attention in what felt like an eternal loop. Trying to look at God within the framework of what I have seen on this Earth kept me from seeing the truth. I needed to unlock my misunderstandings with the key of His love.

Where Was God for You?

If you have never asked this question, now might be a good time to ask it, but not by yourself. Just as I have had many people praying with me to help understand what feels like an overwhelming question, you need the outside perspective of a friend, family member, leader, or pastor.

Spend a few quiet moments praying over these questions:

- Did God let this happen to me, and do I hold Him responsible?
- Have I thought about where God was when I was abused?
- A loving God would not want something bad to happen to me, so where does that leave my relationship with Him?
- Who can I ask for more information regarding this subject?

He Found Me

One day, as I sat reading my Bible, talking to Jesus, He showed me where I had kept Him at arm's length in my life. "Really," I asked. "Not this again, it's okay, I can be okay not knowing where you were. I know you were there somewhere, but it just does not work for me." It all felt too daunting to try to figure out. Honestly, I felt that I did not need to know at this point where God was - there was quiet on the other end of our conversation. It got quieter, and I waited. Deep breath. Then a picture came more and more clearly. Hands were covering my head while horrible acts were happening. Large beautiful hands were covering my head as I attended church, as I spent time at our church youth group, and as I spent time with Jesus. You see, God kept me from remembering what had happened throughout my teen years so that I could find Him and develop a relationship with Him.

This vision, even though a bit overwhelming, did not come with feelings of pain but peace. That is how I discern the difference between a flashback and a vision from God. I am so thankful that throughout over the years, I made the choice to trust God even when I could not picture where He was. My decision to set the right the importance of having Jesus in my life made all the difference in my journey. I decided that getting to know God for who He is and reap all the benefits was more important than wanting to have all the answers. Often, we get so hung up on wanting all the answers that we miss the benefits of just being okay with what we do know. Can you see how it took time for me to be ready to hear what He had to say? Do you see that I needed to put myself in a place that I could hear from Him? I had to be a willing participant.

Have You Found Him?

Have you ever tried to picture God with you, there, while you were raped, sexually molested, or sexually abused? It's difficult. If reading this has your head spinning, I understand, I have felt the same. Give it to Him and let it go. If you get to this spot, He will help you, and it will come with love and ease, not with fear and frustration. Take a deep breath and let God come and be with you. If you need or want to find where God was, ask Him. The Bible says this:

> Here's what I'm saying: Ask and you'll get; Seek and you'll find; Knock, and the door will open.
>
> *Luke 11:9 The Message (MSG)*

Psalm 139 gives us such an incredible example of how to talk to Him:

> God, investigate my life; get all the facts firsthand. I'm an open book to you; even from a distance, you know what I'm thinking. You know when I leave and when I get back; I'm never out of your sight. You know everything, I'm going to say before I start the first sentence. I look behind me, and you're there, then up ahead and you're there, too — your reassuring presence, coming and going. This is too much, too wonderful— I can't take it all in! Is there any place I can go to avoid your Spirit? To be out of your sight? If I climb to the sky, you're there! If I go underground, you're there! If I flew on morning's wings to the far western horizon, you'd find me in a minute — you're already there waiting! Then I said to myself, "Oh, he even sees me in the dark! At night I'm immersed in the light!" It's a fact: darkness isn't dark to you; night and day, darkness and light, they're all the same to you. Oh yes,

you shaped me first inside, then out; you formed me in my mother's womb. I thank you, High God—you're breathtaking! Body and soul, I am marvelously made! I worship in adoration—what a creation! You know me inside and out, you know every bone in my body; You know exactly how I was made, bit by bit, how I was sculpted from nothing into something. Like an open book, you watched me grow from conception to birth; all the stages of my life were spread out before you, the days of my life all prepared before I'd even lived one day. Your thoughts—how rare, how beautiful! God, I'll never comprehend them! I couldn't even begin to count them — any more than I could count the sand of the sea. Oh, let me rise in the morning and live always with you! And please, God, do away with wickedness for good. And you murderers—out of here! — all the men and women who belittle you, God, infatuated with cheap god-imitations. See how I hate those who hate you, God, see how I loathe all this godless arrogance; I hate it with pure, unadulterated hatred. Your enemies are my enemies! Investigate my life, O God, find out everything about me; Cross-examine and test me, get a clear picture of what I'm about; See for yourself whether I've done anything wrong— then guide me on the road to eternal life.

Psalm 139 The Message (MSG)

Just Believe

When I look back, one of the best decisions I made was to believe that God was there even though I could not see Him. The next was to believe that He is a good God. Reading my Bible through this lens helped me realize it did not matter that I couldn't picture where He was when I was abused. As I got older, my faith increased so that when I was ready, God revealed to me that picture of where He was and how He protected me. You can choose Him, too.

Here are some things to know about God:

God is Omnipresent (everywhere at the same time)

Can anyone hide from me in a secret place? Am I not everywhere in all the heavens and earth?" says the Lord.

Jeremiah 23:24 New Living Translation (NLT)

God is Omniscient (knowing everything)

We cannot imagine the power of the Almighty; but even though he is just and righteous, he does not destroy us.

Job 37:23 New Living Translation (NLT)

God is Love (Unconditionally, you do not need to do anything to earn it He takes delight in knowing you)

But anyone who does not love does not know God, for God is love.

1 John 4:8 (NLT)

Understand, therefore, that the Lord your God is indeed God. He is the faithful God who keeps his covenant for a thousand generations and lavishes his unfailing love on those who love him and obey his commands.

Deuteronomy 7:9 (NLT)

Bad Things Happen to Good People

It isn't just you. It isn't just me. Bad things happen to everyone. However, when it happens to us, we think no one understands our pain. God, your Father, understand and cares. When Jesus, His Son, was here on Earth, He was tortured and killed; He understands pain. Yet He also performed countless incredible miracles.

The following story of healing happens after many years of this woman trying doctors of all kinds and what seemed at the time to be the practical way to approach overcoming health ailments. With every try, she was met with failure. Until one day – she met Jesus. She chose to believe the rumors that He was who people said He was, THE ANSWER. In one moment in His presence, with one touch of his clothes, her prayers were answered. I am this woman; We are this woman, in one moment with Jesus.

A woman who had suffered a condition of hemorrhaging for twelve years—a long succession of physicians had treated her, and treated her badly, taking all her money and leaving her worse off than before—had heard about Jesus. She slipped in from behind and touched his robe. She was thinking to herself, "If I can put a finger on his robe, I can get well." The moment she did it, the flow of blood dried up. She could feel the change and knew her plague was over and done with. At the same moment, Jesus felt energy discharging from him. He turned around to the crowd and asked, "Who touched my robe?" His disciples said, "What are you talking about? With this crowd pushing and jostling you, you're asking, 'Who touched me?' Dozens have touched you!" But he went on asking, looking around to see who had done it. The woman, knowing what had happened, knowing she was the one, stepped up in fear and trembling, knelt before him, and gave him the whole story. Jesus said to her, "Daughter, you took a risk of faith, and now you're healed and whole. Live well, live blessed! Be healed of your plague.

Mark 5:25-34 The Message (MSG)

Can you see Him saying to you, "Daughter" or "Son?" He loves you more than you will ever understand on this Earth. We can choose to believe, experience His presence, get ahold of His hem, and get our miracle now. You can welcome His presence right now. You can experience the joy of knowing Him. You can be as this woman was – healed! Jesus is the key; we all need to unlock those things that have kept us from healing.

Jesus Meets Us on Our Side

Before meeting this desperate woman, Jesus was on His way somewhere else to heal a different person. But He stopped. He noticed, and He healed her, too. She wasn't sure He would. There was no "money-back guarantee" for her this time. Taking a chance paid off. Her faith changed her immediately.

God wants to heal you. You don't have to know where He was or where He is. You don't have to understand Him at all because He already understands you. God can help you in this present, to understand your past, so that you can have an incredible future!

In a Cage

Take a moment and look at the front cover art of this book. The person is sitting in a cage. The cage symbolizes how the effects of abuse in our lives can keep us prisoner, even if we could seemingly stand up and walk right out on our own. People say that, too, don't they? Or they leave us with the impression that we should be able to pull up our bootstraps, put on our grown-up pants, and try harder. You name it and I've heard it. People love to accuse, don't they? Why can't you move on? Was it that bad? So what, bad things happen, get over it. And on, and on. When people don't know what to say, they say what was said to them – this doesn't make it right or easy to hear. BUT GOD - Jesus does not do this to us.

In praying for the completion of this book, the cover art kept coming into my mind over and over as I prayed for those of you who would read it. I kept praying for you to come out of your cage into healing. But what Jesus showed me is that He doesn't expect you to get up and climb out on your own. He climbs into the cage with you and sits down. With His help, when you are ready to kneel, He kneels with you. When you are ready to stand, He will stand in the cage with you for as long as you need Him to. One step at a time, there He is, encouraging you, reminding you of His love and offering His strength to you in whatever capacity you need. That is what His love is like – ALWAYS. He did this for me. He had no expectations except wanting to share the journey. He had no requirement except surrender. He brought no conviction, only love, always love.

Exchange Old Locks for New Keys

Old Locks	New Keys
God let this happen to me	I'm no longer a slave to another person's sin *Galatians 5 The Message (MSG)*
God didn't protect me	I am still alive and able to move forward. God is with me *Hebrews 13:5-6 The Message (MSG)*
I can't trust God	God is trustworthy and I choose to trust Him *Proverbs 3:5-6 (NLT)*
My feelings direct my thoughts	Jesus, who lives inside of me, is the filter for my thoughts *Romans 12:2 (NLT)*

Moment with God

God, please help me. I want to allow you to work in me, to heal me so I can move forward. It's okay if I don't understand everything that has happened in my life. Thank you for understanding me. Help me, Lord, to rest in your presence and let you shoulder my cares. In Jesus Name, Amen

From the Inside Out - Our Journey Together

I hope reading this book has helped you on your journey toward healing. My prayer for you is that you have the desire and ability to open yourself up to God, because I know that He is there, ready, willing, and able to heal you. My hope for you is that you will not only find freedom along this path but will continue to let God into your life more and more. In mourning what you have lost, don't pick up those losses again, leave them with Jesus. After you have let yourself be angry, allow yourself to let your anger go too. The health of your soul is more important than holding on to a grudge. Knowing who our true enemy is in this world can make all the difference in being able to forgive others and yourself. Not tolerating irresponsibility but allowing yourself to let go of the blame. Decide to live your life, from here on out, with your hands wide open to Jesus. Give Him all things you've held on to in the past and receive His goodness. Have confidence that He will give you a fresh perspective and bring you joy. Walk with people in your life that encourage you to gain wisdom. Spend time with alone with God so that you gain a firm understanding of who He made you to be. Self-awareness is a gift God gives us when we are ready to receive it. If you are still not able to envision where God was in your past, be okay with this, and if He showed you that He has brought you this far – that is enough. Our Father in heaven, He has everything we could ever need to do the things we want to do and can do here on Earth. You are amazing, God already knows it and He wants you to believe it, too!

My Journey Continues

God is still working on me. Hardly ever any more do I experience debilitating flashbacks. Knowing myself now, I avoid certain movies, books, and people that would influence me wrongly. Keeping my heart guarded and spending time with Jesus helps me stay in the right space. Am I perfect? No. I could give you a list of areas that need improvement. However, I am much more gracious toward myself than I have ever been in my entire life. The acceptance I have for myself and others brings lightness and ease to my life, exactly my hope for you.

Through the journey of writing this book and sharing with others, I kept telling myself, "I'm taking back ground that was stolen from me." Meaning, I thought I was gaining back parts of my life that I should've had the opportunity to enjoy. What I did not realize is that each time I had this thought, a little bit of fear snuck in: fear that I wasn't enough and feared that I could not do what I felt God calling me to do. Driving home one night, not realizing this fear was there, I let the thought linger again, telling myself, "I am taking back the stolen ground." Then tears started to roll down my face as all those little bits of fear hit me all at once like a huge wave. As I cried, I heard His voice. Jesus said, "Why do you think you have to take back the ground? The ground belongs to me. All you must do is walk on the ground that I've given you. The ground is laid out before you full of my grace (unearned favor) so walk, just walk." Incredible amounts of peace followed that conversation. The empowerment that God gave me through my tears at that moment has enabled me to share in these pages what had been my lifelong secret. The truth truly does set us free.

Your Journey

No matter where you are in your journey, God is with you and wants to help you. If you have read this book, not believing that what worked for me will work for you, I get it. I encourage you to go back and revisit one chapter, for example, "Perspective." Each day, for one or two weeks, ask God to change your thinking in one area related to the abuse you suffered. Just one thing. Test it out – talk to God about it and commit to only a short time. And, make it easy – tell yourself "when I have breakfast, coffee, tea, etc. each morning, I'm going to have this conversation with God at the same time every day." Determine to focus on that one thing for your own benefit. Often, we expect ourselves to change completely overnight, but don't. Be patient with yourself. I encourage you to try this with each chapter, but even if you only work on one thing at a time, God can work with that. When you utilize courage and open up to God, He will help you.

God's Desire

Have you ever seen a television show with an episode where a child is kidnapped? Distraught parents wring their hands and are willing to do whatever it takes to get their baby back. Law enforcement agencies spend sleepless nights looking for clues that could lead to the captor. Parents pursue their children. The good parents in these episodes do not give up looking for their child until they are back together.

We have a Father like that. God desires to have a deep relationship with us, one where He meets our needs. He wants us to rely on Him. God's pursuit of us never changes. There is nothing we can do that will keep Him from wanting us to turn towards Him. He wants to hear his children's voices calling His name so that He can save them from their captor. You'll never need another hero, ever.

Where to Go from Here?

No one was meant to do life alone. We were created by God to be in relationship, not just with one another but also with Him. Support to make it through this life, and especially on the journey to freedom from the effects of abuse, is a necessity. Who are your people? The ones you want on this journey are those who encourage you. A counselor? A counseling group? A trusted, reliable friend? A pastor? A mentor? Here's something to pay attention to: how do you feel after you leave these people? Do you feel like you are amazing and could conqueror the world? It's good to evaluate our friendships. We can't get rid of our family because God gave them to us first. However, we can add good people outside of that circle that can help us. Take the time to evaluate who you are listening to and how what they're saying makes you feel.

Input – there's no way around it, our input needs to be managed. We live in a world of bombardment. Pornography and soft-pornography, rated R movies, some rated PG-13 movies, television, the internet, our phones – it all needs to be filtered. Draw a thick line for yourself of where filtering input fits or doesn't fit into your life. Even if you make a short goal of a month where you don't watch rated R movies, my guess is you will feel a huge difference. Add some encouraging music, a Ted Talk, and a great podcast to your days. Find some on my website at **theresareiff.com**.

My Prayer for You

Father in heaven, help each reader of this book to find more of you in each day. Help them to open up their heart to receive your love, your grace (unmerited favor), and your presence. Give your chosen child the same freedom that I have found. Thank you for all the goodness you will bring! In Jesus' name, Amen.

Cited Works

Beaumont, Leland R., Emotional Competency.com, Leland R. Beaumont, 2005-2009, **www.emotionalcompetency.com**

Wendell E and Virginia Smith, The Rhema Book, 2008, Kirkland, WA, The City Church, pages 324-375.

Chandler, Otis, Franklin D. Roosevelt Quotes, Good Reads.com, Good Reads, January, 2007, **https://www.goodreads.com/quotes/51440-in-the-truest-sense-freedom-cannot-be-bestowe-it-must**

Wolfelt, Alan, Grieving vs. Mourning, TAPS, Grieving vs. Mourning, Tragedy Assistance Program for Survivors, 1994, **https://www.taps.org**

Dr. Henry Cloud and Dr. John Townsend, Boundaries, 1992, 2017, Grand Rapids, MI, Zondervan, Epub Edition, location 30

Winfrey, Oprah, Oprah Winfrey Quotes, Good Reads.com, Good Reads January 2007, **https://www.goodreads.com/quotes/84-turn-your-wounds-into-wisdom**

Acknowledgments

Jesus Christ – without you, I would have discarded and discredited myself completely. Thank you for being not only my Savior but also a friend like no other. You filled the holes in my heart that were large enough to engulf me. Thanks, is not enough. I surrender ALL.

Joel Reiff – To my husband, partner for life, my loving best friend; your jokes still make me laugh, and there is no one I'd rather be on this journey with! Thank you for being a fantastic Business Manager and Editor-in-Chief. This book would not exist without you!

Emma Reiff – To my very first baby – I love you deeply and am so proud of the sweet, creative woman that you are! Thank you so much for the perfect cover art. The way you listened to my concept and created this book's cover (and put up with all my changes) was incredible! You are my favorite Emma!

Anna Reiff – My tiniest sweet middle baby daughter – you amaze me. Since your first days, your strength has me in awe. I know God has huge plans for you! I wish that would mean you'll be living right next door (and still might daily pray that you do) but we know when God calls us, we go wherever that is! Love you with all my heart; you are my favorite Anna!

Ally Reiff – I prayed for five years to have another baby because God told me we still needed to add to our family. There you came, and you were everybody's baby to hold and love! Our sweet third baby, you possess a strength both inside and out that is a gift directly from Heaven. I love how you lead everywhere you go, with grace and integrity. I love you so much that I want to kiss your whole face and squeeze you forever! You are my favorite, Ally!

Dot Tubach – Thank you for doing the right thing in a near-impossible situation. I am so proud of you and all that you have overcome. I love you and am so happy for what God has restored in your life.

Alycia Thornton – Sis, there is no one that I enjoy time laughing with more than you. The way that when we are together, it's just like it always has been, so good for my soul. Our uncanny ability to laugh every single time we lift something heavy together might be bizarre but it's us! We'll never own a bakery together because I don't think anyone will buy a pineapple cake with all "backs" to it! I've cried more tears with you than anyone else and we are both still here together thanks to Jesus. Boston to Austin is just geography – sisters no matter where we find ourselves. I love you greatly!

Wendi and Matt Thornton, *Christ Community Church, East Taunton, MA* – I never thought, Matt, that when you married Wendi, I would gain a best friend. The two of you together make up an incredible spiritual force for the kingdom of God. Wendi, you helped keep my foundation firm all these years by your faithful encouragement, honest words and love – my love for you goes deep. Matt, when you were little, I couldn't have imagined what God would do – so very proud of the man, husband, father, friend and pastor you have become – I love you big time!

Liz Matthews – Thank you for your detailed eyes on this book and for being so encouraging along the way. Your timely texts arrive each tie I have needed them the most! Looking forward to a future in ministry together. Love ya!

Made in the USA
Middletown, DE
07 September 2023

38105303R00073